Brother John

Why Are The Fishermen Eating The Bait?

PUBLISHED by PARABLE
Earthly Stories with a Heavenly Meaning

Pathways To The Past

Each volume stands alone as an Individual Book
Each volume stands together with others
to enhance the value of your collection

Build your Personal, Pastoral or Church Library
Pathways To The Past contains an ever-expanding list of
Christendom's most influencial authors

Augustine of Hippo
Athanasius
E. M. Bounds
John Bunyan
Brother Lawrence
Jessie Penn-Lewis
Bernard of Clairvaux
Andrew Murray
Watchman Nee
Arthur W. Pink
Hannah Whitall Smith
R. A. Torrey
A. W. Tozer
Jean-Pierre de Caussade
Thomas Watson
And many, many more.

Tiitle: Why Are The Fishermen Eating The Bait?
Brother John Foy
Rights: All Rights Reserved
ISBN 978-1-945698-03-3
Doctrinal theology, Inspiration
Salvation, Dicipleship, Spiritual Warfare
Other books by this author include: Lovesick

Brother John

WHY ARE THE FISHERMEN EATING THE BAIT?

PUBLISHED by PARABLI
Earthly Stories with a Heavenly Meaning

DEDICATION

    This book is dedicated to the life and memory of my mother in law, Nell Rand. Mother; as we all affectionately called her, had many favorites. She always stated to all 7 daughters, son in laws, all 29 grandchildren and 5 great grandchildren, "You are one of my favorites." Her heart was about family and she loved Jesus. She went to rest in November 2012 and she is greatly missed. She knew about this book for many years and often we would discuss thoughts and ideas that ended up in this book. When returning from any mission's trip she was always present in our house for a few days. After several trips I finally asked her, "Why are you always here when I get back?" She told me, "Because this is when you are your best. I love seeing the passion and desire for the lost and nations on you when you get home."

    I miss that and of course now living abroad, I miss her and the love she showered on my children. She was a woman of peace and love. She helped me become a better husband and never judged me for my mistakes. She was Mother in all lovely and honorable sense of that word.

    Mother I look forward to crossing over and sharing the rest of the story with you! With all love and affection I thank God you were part of our lives for so many years. Thanks for filling that spot that was empty and never will be again. I may have gained a wife but I also gained another Mother.

Author's Preface

My friend, please do not read this and use the Word and Scripture contained with it as a weapon against others. The Word is a sword for use against powers of darkness and not brother and sisters in Christ. I hope and pray that these words written convey my heart for the coming revival and last days harvest that many of us have been praying, fasting and digging in for, some for decades.

After much fasting and prayer I was led to Jeremiah 3:3, Jeremiah 5:24 and 6:16. The common theme being that we have prayed for but not seen the promised harvest rain. I believe the time is right, but sin holds us back. This will be a corporate harvest, not a one man show and therefore the sin of the corporate body must be addressed honestly. Study for yourself and please let Love lead you to your own conclusion.

As for me and my house we will seek Him, and live in a manner that would not prevent His Word from coming to pass in our lives. That is my prayer for The Church as well.

Jeremiah 6:16

16 Thus saith the Lord, Stand ye in the ways, and see, and ask for the old paths, where is the good way, and walk therein, and ye shall find rest for your souls. But they said, We will not walk therein. 17 Also I set watchmen over you, saying, Hearken to the sound of the trumpet. But they said, We will not hearken.

Please my friends harken unto the voice of the Lord our God that it may go well for all of us!

A Place to Start

I have wanted to put this book into publication for over 16 years but I could not bring myself to finish it after many starts and stops. For years I have picked it up only to put it down again, unsatisfied with the overall attitude of it. I in no way want to write anything being critical of others much less brothers and sisters in Christ. But as we approach the last moments here on this planet earth I find a greater cry with- in my heart as well as in the heart of many in the body of Christ.

About the turn of the last century (1900), an older famous preacher was approached by a younger preacher and criticized for how he presented something. The older preacher said to the younger preacher, "Any common ordinary man can criticize another man, but it takes an extraordinary man to edify and lift people up."

My heart in writing this is not to criticize but to edify the Body towards the perfecting of the saints. I want us as the corporate body of Christ to become what we ought (Hebrews 13:20-21) attaining to the fullness of Christ (Ephesians 4). I prefer to believe that what Jesus said in John 17 as He prayed, "that we all may be one as He is and the Father were one." We must as individuals become one with Him and as a corporate body. We are all in this journey together. I know that this book does not apply to every church and individual member of the body, but unfortunately it applies to many.

I want to say that in my life the one thing I strive for is to keep the unity of Love. I would rather remain silent in a room full of spiritual genius's than to break the command of Love. I do my very best to protect my love contact, my vital living contact with the Spirit of God. I don't want anything to interfere with that union. I don't need to write these words but I am compelled to by The Spirit. I have written most of this while fasting and seeking His perfect will in the matter at hand. I want to deliver this in every ounce of love as possible.

I have traveled the world and seen so much good from fellow believers and saints. I have also seen the bad. The world gravitates to the bad. A man can do decades of good work but the world will destroy him over one mistake. My heart is not in that manner here. I want to reach all I can in Christ and for others to go beyond me. I have reached a point in my journey where the Spirit is telling me I cannot go to the hard unreached places anymore. I have to raise them up and send them now. I am accustomed to being in the jungles where it requires a physical effort, where electricity and running water are rumors. I have been poked by little kids who have never seen a white man before and assumed I was a ghost. But I cannot go that hard anymore, and with a large family the expense and cares of this world as a dad have limited me. I have moved into a new season with God that requires being in one place as much as possible. I sorrow to a degree in that but rejoice in my family and that God has provided people we can train up, send, support and love as substitutes. My assignment has changed but the job has not, I may be more logistical now for the body, but we will send as many as possible to the front lines. Jesus told us to pray to Lord of the Harvest to send laborers.

This book is intended to edify and build and help the end time harvesters going to be all they can be in Christ.

The Job and Purpose of the Church

The Primary Job of the Church

As a former drill instructor and having served in combat situations with the 82nd Airborne, I understand that if in combat, the troops follow commands at all costs. If a command is given to "charge" or "take that hill" then everyone charges. (In plain simple terms, this is not the way war is fought anymore.) If in the process, the commanding office dies, the command still stands. Someone else picks up the flag and follows that command, the charge continues. The command does not change until the mission is accomplished. The hill must be taken. The methods may have to adapt or change some but the command to take the hill remains until the mission is complete. If the hill is not taken and a superior officer arrives on the scene to find out why it was not accomplished, even he will go back to the last command. "Why was the hill not taken?" "All of our officers died" might be replied. "But was not the last command to take the Hill?" You see even if the highest ranking or any other officer who gave the command is removed from the battle, the command still stands. You see excuses do not work. Reason does not work. Obedience does. I once heard it said that excuses are just reasons stuffed with lies. When given a command, excuses will not work. The hill must be taken.

Mark 16

15 And he said unto them, Go ye into all the world, and preach the gospel to every creature. 16 He that believeth and is baptized shall be saved; but he that believeth not shall be damned. 17 And these signs shall follow them that believe; In my name shall they cast out devils; they shall

speak with new tongues; 18 They shall take up serpents; and if they drink any deadly thing, it shall not hurt them; they shall lay hands on the sick, and they shall recover.

The last command that Jesus gave was to go into all the world and preach or publish the Gospel. That command still stands today. He said go preach the Gospel and make disciples of all nations. That is our Hill! The primary job of the church is about redemption, about none perishing and making disciples.

Matthew 28

18 And Jesus came and spake unto them, saying, All power is given unto me in heaven and in earth.

19 Go ye therefore, and teach all nations, baptizing them in the name of the Father, and of the Son, and of the Holy Ghost 20 Teaching them to observe all things whatsoever I have commanded you: and, lo, I am with you always, even unto the end of the world. Amen.

The amazing thing is that He also said here, and I will be with you until the end! He has not left us alone to fight the battle!

The primary job of the church is to reach the lost and to make disciples. It's about redemption.

For the most part the US has done a better job of doing this than any other nation. We have sent missionaries around the world but in the last days as the love (agape love) of many grows cold, many are being forgotten and left behind. (Even in our own backyard) Interestingly the word wax is used in Revelation. Wax cools from the outside due to the environment on the outside. The pressures of the world are causing many to wax cold. The real problem is an individual heart problem, but there is also a leadership problem.

I once heard that according to Barna Research that America spends more each year on cat food than missions. We obviously spend more each year on buildings and stateside projects than missions. Yet I meet people so often who say "What about America?" Maybe America's problems are not political or social but rather due to the integrity (meaning the same inside as what is outwardly seen) in the Church.

We could pose many more questions but let's just focused on one?

What would happen to the Church in America if the shepherds (leaders) were feeding the church and releasing them to the lost as opposed to what we now see? It is His harvest not ours, they are His sheep not ours.

The Primary Purpose of the Church is Intimacy.

Jesus called Him Father. He is our Father. Our Abba Father, Not just a dad but a Father. He cares about us. He wants to know us and live with us. Jesus said that if we dwell in Him, He and His Father would come make their home in us. This is more than just the endowment of power that the Church received on the day of Pentecost. This is the living creative magnificent God living in us. So close that He cannot be separated. (ONE) Paul called this a great mystery and compared it to marriage. God in you. It is the primary reason for all of creation. Fellowship is not just a friendship but a closeness that exceeds marriage. Isaiah said that "your sons shall marry you", God wants intimate relationship, a knowing, an intense love. God created us not just to worship Him but to be with Him. When a man sees the one for him, he and that woman begin a journey and a courtship that causes them both to do unreasonable things, in the name of love. God did an unreasonable thing in courting you. He gave His Son. We as men will do anything to "get the girl" but will we do anything to get the Creator? Will we pursue Him like we did our wives? Will we dare to do the unreasonable, the challenging, and the uncommon to court God? He has done it for us. What lengths will you go to so as to deepen your relationship with Christ? Can you live without your wife? Can you live without Christ?

Being in ministry and having done numerous missions trips, I have learned that even leading people to the Lord does not matter when it comes to this personal relationship. Even Jesus said there will be many who come to me and say, "Did we not do miracles and wonders in your name?" Preaching to world will produce those things but it does not mean that you are close to the Father. I have heard people say, "That fellow walks in the Spirit." But when you get to know them they are mean, rude, etc... They may walk in miracles, signs and wonders for a time. Or because they preach the Word, faith comes up in those listening and they have a miracle yet the preacher gets the credit. Then isn't it interesting how their stories are from the past not recent NOW stories but without walking in Love they have nothing. Walking in the Love of God the Father is the way. It is the most perfect way. Everything else will disappear but Love will remain. Where do you stand in your personal intimate walk with God? Is He your all and all? Is He your only source? Are you daily making the pursuit of God your most exciting quest? Your life's adventure is in how you pursue Him. How far are you willing to go with Him? How desperately dependent on Him are you? That begins the journey.

Anyone can get on a plane and preach the Gospel and it needs to be done. I personally have been to dozens of countries and preached to well over half a million. But none of that sustains me; it becomes a memory of yesterday. Today I want Him more than anything else in the World. Out of that I still go to other nations and neighborhoods and tell people about Him. I also walk these streets here where I am and commune with Him as I go. I share that personal relationship with others, and often it produces miracles. I call them accidental miracles, the normal Christian life. They are not planned or performed. They don't always happen in a service but often in the streets. My pursuit is not numbers; my pursuit is not a big church, or even a famous Bible training center. My pursuit is Him. It is the best form of infection a man could have. That is the contagion in my life that makes Him real to others. I get alone with Him, and let Him worry about the results.

"The Bible often describes the job of reaching the lost as it relates to farming, but the Word refers to our individual relationship with God as marriage." -- Jerry O Dell

HOUSTON WE HAVE A PROBLEM

Having traveled all over the world, I often meet people who are running with the same passion I have. We sit down and it is like we are long separated family. It is so wonderful to meet men and women giving all too simple obedience and love for God. After several encounters in far corners of the world, I wondered why we do not get to see them more often or even spend more time with them. Well, a simple answer is that they and I would not be the same if we did not keep doing what we were supposed to be doing. God moves people in order to fulfill His purposes. If we stayed together we would grow cold and stale and lose vision for the Harvest. At the same time I have met men and women who I just keep my real desire to myself and say very little. They care more about pedigrees and business methods than Harvest. Often money is their pursuit. We are not of the same company. The number one issue is some doctrine or teaching of men. So we agree on Jesus and I say very little. That does not make me right or them wrong. Then there are those who just seem to be in it for the position and not the mission. I have seen many continue in this pattern and then God is able to work in them to open their eyes to what He wants. God can change anyone. I once heard a man say, "It's a lot easier to steer a moving car than one that is parked." At least many of these men and women are out there, and many do change as they awaken to the real need.

Years ago I was returning from a trip overseas and had just arrived in the US. I was cleaning up and about to head out for a meal at a friend's house. All of a sudden I was in a large field, acres of land. It was about dusk and there were a few others around me in the distance. I looked down and saw marbles all around my feet. Just past the top of my ankles. The entire field was covered in marbles. I saw people picking them up and putting them down. Picking them up and putting them down. So I reached down and grabbed one, I looked at it and thought, "That is neat," then set it back down. After about 3 of these, I found one I really liked and put it in a satchel that was tied around my waste. I repeated this for several minutes; never moving from that spot. I collected some marbles that I thought were great and put back others that did not really appeal to me. After several of these I looked up around the field and a realization occurred to me and I said, "God what is this? It would take me an eternity to look at all these marbles." God replied, "My Son each marble is a truth about me, some you like and keep, some you don't and you put back"

  I would never presume to know everything or think that I have God figured out. I am but a signpost pointing home. I have no desire to insult or hurt anyone but only to keep the peace in love. That being said, there is injustice in the Church and people are getting hurt and we as a church cannot fulfill our destiny unless we fix it. We must do it as individuals and as a corporate body. My heart is that eyes would be opened and hearts would be mended. You and I are not alone. He sees us and where we are. Let's learn from one another and become all that we can. As individuals we must care what is happening to the Church body as a whole as it affects the outcome of the entire Bride of Christ.

  We live in an age where often in private conversation folks will talk about the heresy and sin of church leaders. As a church we are under attack from the left and right for the abuse of the saints in prosperity from the world. It is a constant attack in the media about the values of the church and why they don't matter. We hear people say we are brain washed, and I cannot argue with them. Some leaders of the church have taken advantage of the sheep and acted as hirelings not shepherds. In your own life how many times have you had someone outside the church point out all the problems and wrongs in the Church as a whole? For so long my only answer could be, "Well that is how it should not be and not all churches are that way." But we are a corporate body. We are all part of the same body and I do not like having to face those questions. But it's my own (church) family causing them to be asked. If the world can see it and it is giving them an excuse for acting the way they do, why do we not fix it?

The funny thing is this: how can we blame the world for acting out in a way that is consistent with their nature? We should expect the world to behave this way. How can we defend The Church when it's our leaders who are the ones, preaching and allowing the lack of integrity and character? As a Church, I refer to the whole body, not just that church over there that seemingly has everything right, versus the one across town that just had another pastor have another moral failing. I see the problems and the empowerment of evil in our world not the fault of politicians and well-funded liberal groups but rather the failing of church leaders. (Fulfillment of times and prophecy as well) We cannot expect that the world is going to let up on its attack of the church, when we give them the ammo with which to shoot us. It's our fault. As long as we as individuals in Christ, (also as part of a corporate body of Christ) do not live the standard given to us we will have to give an account, and we cannot and should not expect the world to let up. We are all part of one family and when someone acts in a manner unbecoming of this family, do we stand up for what is true or decide let it go? We must side with truth. The first step in recovery is to identify the problem and accept responsibility for it.

I once heard about two men having lunch after a service. They were discussing the fact that the pastor said something that was not Word. He was wrong and both these men knew it. One said, "Well we need to say something" and the other man said, "I am going to keep quiet and walk in love". Well who was right? Well the first, because you cannot separate truth from love. To say that the second man was right is actually part of the problem. He's not walking in love, but rather inordinate affection. We must side on love (true agape love) which can never be separated from truth. We must walk in the standard God has given us. On the flip side of the coin I know plenty of men and women who know a lot of the Bible and proclaim it as truth, but have no love walk. That truth they want everyone to listen to is actually just knowledge, you cannot separate love and truth, nor can you separate truth from love.

Besides the prophetic outcome and that fact that the world will grow darker in the end; which we see happening. The real problem is not that the world is doing exactly what the Bible says they will do. But is the Church doing what it is supposed to be doing? Are we living to the standard of Jesus? While the world will grow darker, the light is not supposed to grow dimmer but rather brighter. I do not see that meaning that the darker it gets even a dim light appears to shine brightly. The glory of the latter house is supposed to be greater than the former. We in the church spend so much time talking about the end time and we have experts all over who disagree with each other. Everyone in the Church has been well versed on the antichrist. Where are the experts who know what the end time church is supposed to be like? We're supposed to be the overcoming Church in all this end time teaching. Seldom do the end time experts spend more than a brief moment stating, "Don't worry we will be gone". That may be so, but isn't there a job to do first and a harvest to be brought into the barns before that? (Isaiah 60) It will require a different focus to get a different outcome. The outcome God wants. I believe with all my heart that there will be a remnant that will get the job done but I also really believe that as many of us that want it can be part of that end time move.

We as the children of God have a divine purpose and plan for the last days. God has things to be done. We are not supposed to live by fear and yet most of our end time teaching about the end times is focused on what the antichrist will do. We the church are giving the attention to the wrong party! We need to study the Word and see what The Church is supposed to be doing, who the saints are to be and to be doing.

I love the story about the garden when they came to arrest Jesus. (Mark 14, Luke 22 & John 18) They came in boldly with no respect for Him, under the orders of an earthly king, Jesus said, "Whom do you seek?" The soldiers said "Jesus of Nazareth" He answered them, "I AM HE" Then an amazing thing happened. They fell to the ground. He displayed His Power and Glory to them. They had to get up, dust their clothes off and pick up their earthly weapons. Then they had to ask again and this time I doubt they were as bold and disrespectful as the previous attempt. He then went with them. He went on His own accord, not according to what the power of the world wanted.

We are not of this world but we keep doing things like the world. Where is the power (Acts 1:8)? Where is the Glory? It has been stopped by the traditions and teaching of men. We have preached a powerless producing gospel around the world and we have rendered the Church of God with knowledge and great business methods but no power. Most of the church of the world does things according to worldly business methods and techniques. I recall a Scripture, "You have a form of godliness but lack the power there of..." Much like the Jewish church in the day of Jesus, the modern church has lost the presence and thus lost the power! We look like The Church but are falling well short of the intended target.

We have substituted presence and power for world methods and business plans. Jesus himself stated in Mark 10 that we should not do things that way of the world. Doing things in a carnal manner have helped get us to this form of godliness.

Mark 10:42

42 But Jesus called them to him, and saith unto them, Ye know that they which are accounted to rule over the Gentiles exercise lordship over them; and their great ones exercise authority upon them. 43 but so shall it not be among you: but whosoever will be great among you, shall be your minister: 44 and whosoever of you will be the chiefest, shall be servant of all. 45 For even the Son of man came not to be ministered unto, but to minister, and to give his life a ransom for many.

He is also addressing this issue in Matthew 20:22. The word used in the Greek is here is the word diakonos, meaning one who executes the command of another, a steward. Not a lord. I see the words "It shall not be that way among you" as an indictment of the bickering and selfish ambition of the twelve around Jesus. He set them straight. We are not to do things the way the world does them. We should be dependent upon Him not the world's way of doing things. The business plans of the World will not work in The Church.

For example.

I was sitting at a bus stop in a remote part of India years ago. A local pastor was sitting with me and he began to "pull for money". He was good. He went on for a while and I finally looked at him and kind of forcefully asked him where he learned that junk. He looked at me shocked and began to tell me that he learned it from his American sponsor. I had come to India with $200 USD and I was 3 months into my stay and there I was in need and no one knew it. Now here's an Indian pastor taught by Americans how to pull for money, he saw me as a target because I was

WHY ARE THE FISHERMEN EATING THE BAIT?

an American. I have had to go to many places without money. I have been on many "forced fasts" and I did my best to never let anyone know. It was not anyone else's business. It was between me and God. I never starved and I have yet to die. And interestingly enough many people over the years have approached me one on one and apologized for "not listening to the Spirit and giving." Many of those apologies come from the same time frame we were in need. God provided in other ways, but not always as my flesh wanted. My dependency is on God not what man can provide. That pastor was taught the world's way to do things not Jesus dependency.

I was in another remote area and visited a Bible School on the border of Bhutan. I had just been smuggled into Bhutan and some other, "off limit places." I was asked to minister to some students that were going back into Bhutan as underground preachers. If they got caught they would spend 3 months in jail. If they got caught a second time, they were escorted to the border with no papers and not allowed back in. So I went to this Bible school and went into a back room to pray before teaching. As I entered the room I found a dozen rolled up banners. I looked at them and each had a different "Sponsor" name of a different large and popular Church in America. None were the same as the one hanging on the front of the school while I was there. I did a little asking and found out that the banners were changed according to who was coming. That is the type of thing that makes the world mock us. Everyone in that town sees those banners changing and they know what is going on. Those are the type of business practices of the church that ruins the reputation of the body. The same practice goes on today in churches throughout Central America.

We have been to many countries on every continent and we often run into missionaries who have the "do it like America style of ministry." One of my mentors Jerry Odell calls this the "American Gospel." They want the nations to minister to the Lord the way we do in the US. But how is it that America has a better Gospel than anyone else? I meet so many young people who think that by going on a one week trip that they will change the World. I once thought that way. I have a good friend that I have traveled the world with and we have taken many Americans on these trips. We know that after about 3 days into the trip, the young missionaries eyes are beginning to open and we can then help them see the difference between the "American Gospel" and the Living Gospel of Jesus Christ. Taking people out of America is more about Changing America than changing the nations they go to. (Please know that we are aware that not all nations have heard the Gospel and need to hear.) Those front line ministries are not what I'm referring to and I'm not saying that all ministries are like this or that all ministries are missing it, but the world focuses on the ones that are and those doing it right have to bear the damage of these actions. Our assignment currently has us raising up missionaries out of Central and South America to send to front lines. There is a place for crusading, but all ministry needs to be done with integrity.

We have over 4 billion people who need to hear the Gospel. Not a form of godliness but the Gospel. There is a lot of work to be done but we will not get it done operating in the current manner we have perfected.

Here in Central America we meet many missionaries who send pictures home of neglected and pathetic kids and then raise money off those pictures. The nationals know it. They know that missionaries are doing it and they talk about it in their neighborhoods. Oh they'll take the free stuff from any American that brings it to them. They smile and act polite and let the missionaries take their photos. But there is no respect. They do not see them as men of God. They see them as thieves. That is why they treat them the way they do. The nationals can sniff those types of preachers out in a heartbeat. I know before coming to where we are now, we did a lot of research and found many who advertise about what they are doing. One we even knew where he lived. A nice huge house in the US with a private street name "International Harvester" yet we have been unable to figure out exactly where and what he is doing here. He's not where his website says he is. These are just a few examples of things preachers do that hurt the rest of us.

Pastors control the churches and in doing so control the money. I know missionaries doing the right thing and have no support. Pastors fall for the best presentation verses the best. They think these who agree with them are those who they need to support. They are sending out missionaries just as powerless and weak in their relationship with God as they are. It produces a sad cycle that sends the cheapest form of Gospel around the world. A Gospel that produces rich missionaries and pastors while others who are ready sit in the pews and or are forced home

WHY ARE THE FISHERMEN EATING THE BAIT?

from the mission field. Just because you have money to go doesn't make you ready to go. Just because you went to Bible school doesn't mean you're a pastor or a missionary. Being called of God and having a deep personal relationship with Him is the only thing that makes you ready. We must separate out those called by the Spirit as Barnabas and Paul were. Preparation time is not wasted time, but neither is alone time with God developing a foundation of love that will never fail. That being said, it's hard but does not apply to every pastor, church or ministry, but this happens and often when and if we get outside of our bubble of influence we find it ... quickly.

I often tell my boys, it is not what you say about yourself but what other say about you that counts. Others make your testimony. We live it but others lend proof and truth to it.

We must learn to respect ourselves and quit lying to ourselves about the quality of our relationship with God. We must learn to respect the ones we have been sent to and realize not everyone in every country is a dumb native. They often know more than we do. They can be the greatest resource available to help us to accomplish what God may have asked us to do. We need to teach those nationals dependency upon God as we have ourselves pursued Him. We must teach relationship, that is not knowledge. We must teach that ministry is not business. It is the way of Love, Love that cannot fail.

I pray that this book can help solve this problem. God is going to be on the move in a mighty way in the last day and as the latter rain is poured out, I want all of us; as much as possible, to walk in it and spread it and get the job done. I want all to walk in the fullness of Christ and I cannot defend the position that only a preacher can walk in the gifts and power. According to everything I see in the Word all saints are supposed to walk in the highest possible measure of God there is. In today's modern church we have turned preachers into mini gods. We worship them and not God. The flock ends up serving that preacher instead of being served by the ministry gift. Ephesians chapter 4 does a great job of explaining what the job of a minister is; verse 12, for the perfecting of the saints for works of service. Not works of service to a preacher but to God! To the nations that need God!

God never wanted us to have kings and priest over us, but Israel begged for them. There is no need of a mediator between you and Jesus, you can know Him as well as you want. Then you can go back to your corporate Body and help in the perfecting of the rest of the saints, in Love. You know what you have to do to develop that relationship with Christ. Get quiet and let Him minister to you.

But here's the question many ask... Where's the power? I am convinced that the power is not present due to the teachings and doctrines of men. We have been building something other than His kingdom. I know that there are many churches on the right path, but as a whole if one part of the body is failing, aren't we all? God wants us to be healed, filled, and living the fullest life, not a make it to the end life. The current church condition is similar to the condition of the nation of Israel when Jesus walked on the Earth. There is a Levitcal priesthood that the rest of the nation (the church) is serving and yet we seem to have a form of godliness but lack the power there of. We serve priesthood that most are not even aware that there is something missing because they have never experienced the real presence of God. They have experienced the religion.

Generation after generation from the return of the people to Israel and the rebuilding of the Temple were missing something and not knowing it. It is the same today. Many in leadership have no idea that they are missing something and someone. How can those who are blind lead others, except into blindness?

SHEPHERDS

I write this chapter with much fear, as I am a Pastor and I also can fall into the same trappings that others have. I could easily spare a lot of people discomfort by saying that I am referring to spiritual leaders and not just pastors, as we all know that there are many other gifts in the church who are abusing the gifting's and offices given them. Scripture often uses the word pastor or shepherd. So will I. That being said pastors, also called shepherds in the Word hold a vital part to play in the last day. I do not see any other group set apart for what we are going to talk about here, although some times the word elders is used. Our focus here is on Shepherds. It can apply to anyone in leadership of the Church.

Part of the problem lies in the leadership of church. Preachers are not teaching the sheep how to be free and grow to maturity. There may be a multitude of reasons for this but the children of God are not growing into the Sons of God. Point blank... They are stuck in perpetual infancy. Believers are not being fed to grow. Many are being fed enough to make them feel good and safe but not to grow and explore life outside the four walls of their shepherd's corral.

I learned years ago that the best teachers are those who want their students to leave and succeed and do better, go further and faster and higher in success than they ever could or did. A teacher should know that his success is not in what he builds but in the success of those he builds and releases.

We as preachers must preach so they can hear and then feed them the milk and meat of the Word so they become mature. Then they need to be kicked out of the nest to do what God has for them to do. Then if they fail, we bring them back with open arms and love on them. Give them what they need to heal then send them back out. How many times? How about 7 times 70? Why do we praise those who meet some sort of religious success bar but disdain those who don't meet the standards we have set for spiritual success? Why do we use the Word of God as a sword against fellow saints? Why do we not act like our Father who loved us in all our failings as well as successes.

Pastors have the control. They control the money, the sheep and the teaching. For the most part, modern church society has empowered the pastor over the sheep to the point that sheep refuse to grow up and many pastors don't want them to grow. Pastors are not supposed to be CEO's. They are stewards, as Paul said, Love slaves.

I had breakfast with my best friend the other day and we talked about this issue. He pointed out something that got me meditating on this as I drove away. We ministry gifts (pastors, evangelist, prophets, apostles, teachers) are the bottom layer, the foundation of the church. The stones (the sheep) are then laid upon us to build the body. But it seems that the modern church as flipped the model. We have sheep at the bottom supporting the ministers. The ministers in turn lord over the sheep. That was never meant to happen. God only gave Israel a king because they begged for it, He warned them about that.

As I drove away I meditated on what my friend told me. As I meditated a thought developed in me. There seems to be three kinds of pastors/leaders, Jeremiah talks about pastors who are really a type of civil authority, they manage the moral decline of a society. The powers at be need them to slow the moral decay of a generation down enough to keep it from being noticeable. These ministers are often raised in the church and told by family for years they need to be ministers. They go to Bible school and get jobs and careers in ministry but have no calling. They borrow sermons and topics from others to even get something together for service. There is no "Now" revelation. They have no love for the sheep and we might even call them hirelings.

Then there are pastors who hold the office of pastor. They have a driver's personality and get a lot done. They do a good job as a pastor but they miss the relationship required to make it real. They can produce large followings with all the modern atmosphere tools and tricks of the trades. They require great marketing schemes and budgets to make things work. They can teach, they can produce other ministers. They may have a calling but they are missing the heart of the matter. They often see themselves as the "anointed man of God". These men "lord" over the sheep. They do not know that something is missing; they do not know that the Presence of God is missing.

Then there are pastors, or shepherds. They break at night for the sheep They understand the words of Solomon, "I cried on my pillow". They feed the sheep, they seek no reward, they heal the wounds, and they bind up the broken hearted. These servants care; they give to the flock and then spend time in the closet crying out for more. These shepherds stay up at night watching for the promise, they pray, they love. They understand and walk in the revelation of Agape Love. They carry a shepherd's staff, not a rod. They toil where no one notices. They have a "Now" relationship, they are dependent upon Him and Him alone. These wonderful people see God's children as the "anointed of God" They know something is not right in the system we have but may not know it is the lack of power, the lack of Presence because it has been hidden from them. They are looking!

Shepherd's should care, be assessable, lowly and not high minded. They want the sheep to become all they can be. They depend on Jesus and want others to be dependent upon Him as well. They do not exalt themselves but exalt others. They are humble wonderful men. They may not get everything right.

The job of the ministry gift is not to make the children of God dependent on a man, or a church or a doctrine, but dependent on Jesus. To teach, train, and send others out into works of service for the Kingdom.

Eph 4: 9

11 And he gave some, apostles; and some, prophets; and some, evangelists; and some, pastors and teachers; 12 For the perfecting of the saints, for the work of the ministry (does this mean all saints to work of ministry?) for the edifying of the body of Christ:13 Till we all come in the unity of the faith, and of the knowledge of the Son of God, unto a perfect man, unto the measure of the stature of the fullness of Christ:14 That we henceforth be no more children, tossed to and fro, and carried about with every wind of doctrine, by the sleight of men, and cunning

craftiness, whereby they lie in wait to deceive; 15 But speaking the truth in love, may grow up into him in all things, which is the head, even Christ: 16 From whom the whole body fitly joined together and compacted by that which every joint supplied, according to the effectual working in the measure of every part, maketh increase of the body unto the edifying of itself in love.

God wants not one to be an infant. He wants us all to grow into maturity and become what He has for each of us to be- The fullness of Christ. But we cannot grow into maturity as individuals and as a corporate body if the preachers continue to abuse and neglect the most important job within the church, maturing the saints to perfection to the fullest measure of Christ. I am aware that this is a blanket statement but the point is made that we are not just individuals but part of a larger body. We could say that maturity in Christ is total dependency upon Christ.

How can you expect a child to grow if you feed him junk food? The junk food is the teaching of men and the craftiness of men. Feed the meat. Love, Spirit, Truth

The job of any spiritual gifting to the church is to perfect the saints, specifically to build them up and send them out. Not to make the people serve them in endless ministry projects. But to teach them, feed them meat and then kick them out of the nest into what God has for them. We preachers must become the servants of the people. We must teach them to hear the voice of the great Shepherd and to listen to His voice before ours. We must teach them to follow Him, not us and our doctrine.

The Current Conditions

Let's look at what the prophets say about the condition of the church today

Zechariah 10
1 Ask ye of the Lord rain in the time of the latter rain; so the Lord shall make bright clouds, and give them showers of rain, to every one grass in the field. 2 For the idols have spoken vanity, and the diviners have seen a lie, and have told false dreams; they comfort in vain: therefore they went their way as a flock, they were troubled, because there was no shepherd. 3 Mine anger was kindled against the shepherds, and I punished the goats:

In the time frame given here, the time of the latter rain implies harvest. He mentions grass. That is not just fields of grass but "to every one grass in the field." Also the latter day or the last day, well there is no other day after this current one, so he must be speaking about this time and hour.

Revelation 9: 4
"And it was commanded them that they should not hurt the grass of the earth, neither any green thing, neither any tree; but only those men which have not the seal of God in their foreheads."

BROTHER JOHN

The implication here is that the grass, any green thing, and any tree is referring to men. It finishes out by saying but only those men which have not the seal of God in their foreheads. He isn't referring to grass and trees in first part of the sentence and then start talking about men in the last part. He goes on to explain that there are idols that speak. Idols that speak? That caught my curious eye. So I did a word search and only found one other idol that speaks in the entire Word of God that being the idol of the false prophet in Daniel. But this word for idols here in Zechariah is used only twice in the entire Bible. (idols Hebrew 8655 meaning family images or family idols, used in 1 Samuel 15:23 but does not speak) This indicates something different to me, considering that there are over other 100 references to idols in the Word. Most are all the same meaning in the Hebrew or Greek. And interestingly enough this idol referred to here- speaks! It is a family Idol. This idol speaks lies, vanities and false dreams... What do we know of, that presents us with fantasy and false dreams and vanity? Why are our kids so vain? What out there in the day of the latter rain, (remember he is a prophet looking forward in time) gives us false hope and speaks deceit. If I was a prophet looking forward into this day and age I think this is how I would describe what most of us all have in the main room of our house and it is the center of attention in most living rooms- televisions! Now let me be careful to say that I do not see television as evil or that technology is but I see the talking heads on the news, Hollywood and its glamorous appeal as what the prophet saw. He saw something like a news cast or someone who had the appearance or image of man speaking.

And look how he goes into it further. They (the media) GIVE VAIN COMFORT. How many times have we just wanted to escape our problems and sorry excuse of a day by turning on the Television and turning ourselves off and zoning on the TV. When we should be going to God and His Word in need of comfort and encouragement we are going to our family idols and getting false comfort and lies. We are feeding our spirits with lies and vanity when we should be eating the manna of God. Faith cometh by hearing, it works for the lies and deceit just as well as the Word of God. We have given our faith potential to the media instead of God!

And what happened to the sheep, to the congregations? One version of the word says, they wander like sheep without a shepherd. The church as a body has many who are lost, confused, separated, and ignorant. Maybe not you specifically but that means you need to lead others out. Sheep are pretty stupid animals and very defenseless. The prophet goes on to blame one group of people, the shepherds or as we call them today the pastors. His anger will burn against the pastors.

The sad thing is that many pastors are doing all they can with all they know to do. Without the Spirit and Power (you received power when the Holy Spirit comes upon you) they are powerless and confused as the sheep. But the shepherds are supposed to be the leaders of the sheep. They are supposed to warn them and guide them into maturity. Most pastors are not mature because they were taught what they know by someone who was just a powerless as them. So year after year and day after day we produce powerless leaders, who blindly led sheep into this wandering state. They just do all they can to keep their sheep from going to another Shepherd's corral. I would rather close our church doors than be this way.

When will pastors take account for this? When will they realize they are doomed to judgment for this conduct? You might say I'm being hard on pastors but have we not in our current church condition lifted pastors up to the top of the church? Do they not control the vision and direction of the most churches teaching this vain gospel? Do not many men and women with a call of God go into pastoring because it seems more comfortable and smooth? Pastors are unfortunately going to be judged harshly. Let's examine that.

There are many warnings about Shepherds leading the flock away from God.

EZK 34

1 And the word of the Lord came unto me, saying, 2 Son of man, prophesy against the shepherds of Israel, prophesy, and say unto them, Thus saith the Lord God unto the shepherds; Woe be to the shepherds of Israel that do feed themselves! Should not the shepherds feed the flocks? 3 Ye eat the fat, and ye clothe you with the wool, ye kill them that are fed: but ye feed not the flock. 4 The diseased have ye not strengthened, neither have ye healed that which was sick, neither have ye bound up that which was broken, neither have ye brought again that which was driven away, neither have ye sought that which was lost; but with force and with

cruelty have ye ruled them. 5 And they were scattered, because there is no shepherd: and they became meat to all the beasts of the field, when they were scattered. 6 My sheep wandered through all the mountains, and upon every high hill: yea, my flock was scattered upon all the face of the earth, and none did search or seek after them.

7 Therefore, ye shepherds, hear the word of the Lord; 8 As I live, saith the Lord God, surely because my flock became a prey, and my flock became meat to every beast of the field, because there was no shepherd, neither did my shepherds search for my flock, but the shepherds fed themselves, and fed not my flock; 9 Therefore, O ye shepherds, hear the word of the Lord; 10 Thus saith the Lord God; Behold, I am against the shepherds; and I will require my flock at their hand, and cause them to cease from feeding the flock; neither shall the shepherds feed themselves anymore; for I will deliver my flock from their mouth, that they may not be meat for them.

Here we see the shepherds getting fat off the sheep. The shepherds take all they want and leave the sheep to wander. They become sick and weak. Jesus said he came to heal the sick and bind up the broken hearted, to preach deliverance to the captives, but here we see that the shepherds are not doing it. (Luke 4) Many have wandered away and the shepherds do not pursue them. Then in verse 7, the warning begins. I wonder how many people would want to pastor if we started training them here in this verse. According to the Word of God, he saw a day coming when shepherds would do exactly opposite of what Jesus said in Luke 4 He came to do.

Please note that I would agree with anyone who says to me, well aren't there evangelist on TV doing the same thing. Yep, prophets, self-proclaimed apostles and teachers as well. So you could say I am an equal opportunity critic. I keep using the word shepherd and pastor because that is what most all these Scriptures I quote use.

Years ago I heard about a pastor who week after week stood in his pulpit and said "I thank God for a million dollars." Well, after a year of this a fellow in the church decided to give the pastor a million dollars. He made the mistake of telling the pastor ahead of time that he was going to sell a parcel of land that should get a few million easily. This gentleman decided to put the parcel of land up to auction with no reserve. Surely thinking it was going to sell for the appraised value. Well the night before the auction it snowed and very few showed up for the event. The land sold for well under a million dollars. The gentleman wanted to keep his word so He took the check of less than a million to the pastor. The pastor said "That's fine you can owe me the rest!"

That pastor's heart was revealed and the manipulation was exposed. Are you familiar with the story of Jacob and the spotted sheep and cows? Jacob put a principle to work and by making the sheep and cows eat and drink daily in front of the spots reeds and sticks, over a period of time the offspring of those animals became spotted. Jacob ended up with more than his father in law. This pastor put that principle in to use by saying every service that someone was going to give him one million dollars and it produced that in one of the sheep. But the pastor's heart was greed and nothing more. That is not the Spirit of God.

That is abuse of the flock. That is a foolish pastor...

Zechariah 11:15

And the Lord said unto me, Take unto thee yet the instruments of a foolish shepherd. 16 For, lo, I will raise up a shepherd in the land, which shall not visit those that be cut off, neither shall seek the young one, nor heal that that is broken, nor feed that that standeth still: but he shall eat the flesh of the fat, and tear their claws in pieces. 17 Woe to the idol shepherd that leaveth the flock! The sword shall be upon his arm, and upon his right eye: his arm shall be clean dried up, and his right eye shall be utterly darkened.

Zechariah 11 is a prophetic look at Jesus the good Shepherd who was rejected and a foolish shepherd that will come to an end. It seems in verse 16 he states that he knew ahead of time that shepherds would rise up one day and treat the church in the current manner, it does not end well for those shepherds.

One day I was driving down the road in North Carolina and unction to pray came over me. I pulled over and began to pray and was led to Ezekiel 8 and 9. As I began to read it seemed as if this story jumped off the pages at me. I began to cry and pray for the Church as I gained understanding of what those verses meant. I saw the elders of the church who bow down to the idols of the east (Ezekiel 8:12-17). It says they turn their backs on the temple and face the east and bow down. Which is a complete opposite of the tabernacle God instructed Moses to build; you had to turn your back on the east (World way of doing things) to face the Tabernacle holding that Ark and then walk through the gate with your back turned on the world. The high priest always backed out of the Holy Of Holies. He did not turn his back on God, on the altar of God, on the presence of God. Later in chapter 9, He sent a scribe to mark those who have not bowed down to the eastern god. He told the scribe to place a mark on the head of each one who did not bow down to the idols of the east. (Ezekiel 9:4) In 9:5-6 he orders all those who have this mark of The Spirit (see Rev 9:4 as well) to be left alone but to kill the rest, beginning in the sanctuaries. He strikes down the elders first, that allowed it to happen.

I see this as a specific sign of the churches bowing down and mixing Islam with the Christian Church. It will not go well for those leaders who allowed this to happen. Those men who allow this to happen will not live out their days. It is in the Word. I know people say there is a rapture coming, if it does, these men will fall beforehand. God's word is true. They will be stuck down not taken out.

Foolish leaders have a form of godliness but lack the presence there of...

THE GOOD SHEPHERD IN COMPARISION

Psalm 23:

1 The Lord is my shepherd; I shall not want. 2 He maketh me to lie down in green pastures: he leadeth me beside the still waters. 3 He restoreth my soul: he leadeth me in the paths of righteousness for his name's sake. 4 Yea, though I walk through the valley of the shadow of death, I will fear no evil: for thou art with me; thy rod and thy staff they comfort me. 5 Thou preparest a table before me in the presence of mine enemies: thou anointest my head with oil; my cup runneth over. 6 Surely goodness and mercy shall follow me all the days of my life: and I will dwell in the house of the Lord forever.

A good shepherd makes sure his sheep are fed, protected, all their needs are met. It reminds me of the apostle of the early days, in Acts 2: 42-47 where they gathered together and broke bread together and everyone shared their common supply. And they saw miracles sign and wonder and they grew daily. A good shepherd lays his wants and desires down for the good of the flock. He stands guard over them and makes sure they are safe. He does not lord over them but empowers them through solid biblical teaching to become what God wants them to become. A real Shepherd follows the same principle of Jesus, "He does what he sees the Father do and He says what He hears the Father say and reserves judgment for Himself and Himself alone."

Mat 9:36

36 But when he saw the multitudes, he was moved with compassion on them, because they fainted, and were scattered abroad, as sheep having no shepherd. 37 Then saith he unto his disciples, The harvest truly is plenteous, but the labourers are few; 38 Pray ye therefore the Lord of the harvest, that he will send forth labourers into his harvest. Similar to Mark 6:34

John 10: 11

I am the good shepherd: the good shepherd giveth his life for the sheep. 12 But he that is an hireling, and not the shepherd, whose own the sheep are not, seeth the wolf coming, and leaveth the sheep, and fleeth: and the wolf catcheth them, and scattereth the sheep. 13 The hireling fleeth, because he is a hireling, and careth not for the sheep. 14 I am the good shepherd, and know my sheep, and am known of mine. 15 As the Father knoweth me, even so know I the Father: and I lay down my life for the sheep. 16 And other sheep I have, which are not of this fold: them also I must bring, and they shall hear my voice; and there shall be one fold, and one shepherd.

He is the good shepherd and His sheep know his voice.

Did you know that during Bible times many shepherds would share a corral at night? The shepherd would lie down at the gate to sleep. There was no other way into the corral. And in the morning each shepherd would get up and call his sheep out from among the rest of the sheep in the corral. Each shepherd would do this until each had his own flock. Jesus' sheep know His voice. Shepherds must teach their sheep to hear His voice. He also points out that there are hirelings. Listen folks hirelings want one thing, the money. They don't care about the masters sheep, they care about the paycheck, the comfort it brings. A true shepherd has compassion and then feeds them and cares for them. Jesus is the true shepherd.

One thing is clear, if you want to be a shepherd you might want to count the cost. If we presume to be teachers, we better check ourselves and what we are teaching. I love Deuteronomy 28. It begins by saying, If you will listen to the voice of the Lord" and "if you will obey my commands" which for the New Testament believer is being led by the Spirit (Romans 8:14) and the command of John 13:34 to walk in love, at all cost, that is how the world will know we are His disciples. Then and only then will the blessings of God overtake you. Be led and walk in Love!

As a former soldier I understand a little of the need to follow orders and get the job done. Since leaving the military and college I have been in the seemingly endless business of helping others accomplish what God has told to them do. It all comes down to reaching the lost and as far as I am concerned, the lost are those who do not know Jesus. If your mission was to preach the Gospel I wanted to help. I would do anything I could to help others, often teaching all I knew. Then going with them on trips and demonstrating that Word in action. But not everyone is willing to do it at all costs. I often found myself butting heads with preachers who had it all figured out and I would just keep my tongue and act as if I knew nothing. Many of them had a nice easy path that they have followed and when we speak of miracles, signs, and wonders and the manifested presence of God they freak. I often ran into men who have the position of a pastor and have a church full of people, many of who are powerless and imprisoned by the pastor.

My wife and I had dinner with one of these types of pastors, not much older than us and he made a lot of lofty comments and promises to us. Then after he talked himself out, he actually said three things in that conversation that struck me as interesting. "You both have such great faith; I wish my people had that kind of faith." A compliment? Scary sign number one. Later he said "My people are so head strong they are missing the spirit of it." Scary sign #2. Then came the final scary one "You both are not ready, you need to stay here and learn under me for a few years!" The old drill instructor in me managed to not lay hands on him suddenly. Unfortunately, that pastor did not live out his life to an

WHY ARE THE FISHERMEN EATING THE BAIT?

old age. His books are everywhere and he is in the grave. He left behind a family and church that could have changed the world. It was said of this pastor at his funeral, "He had skin like that of an old badger"... Really?! Those who knew him might be more honest and say he was just plain mean. There seemed to be a vital missing part of his walk with God, the Love walk.

Where was the love? Did he not tell us what the problem with his church was? They were head strong. Doesn't that indicate something in the food is causing that? Most people who got to know him talked about how intelligent he was, so much so you could hardly understand his books. A church built around the personality of the pastor will act like the pastor.

Years ago I was at a convention with fellow missionaries.

A somewhat famous preacher was invited and I had never seen him before and had no idea who he was. As he began to speak I kept hearing, me, mine, I, my stuff etc.., and all this stuff that was supposed to indicate that he was some big shot. As he walked to the left side of the church, I then saw him lifted above the crowd to the right side. In this vision, I started at the top, his hair was perfect, his suit gleamed, his gold watch and rings shone, his pants were perfectly starched, and everything was perfect. Then his shoes... no he had no shoes. He had hairy split hoofs that made me recoil. I almost threw up and when I recoiled the SPIRIT OF GOD said to me "How beautiful are the feet of those who carry my Gospel." I got up and walked out the door and as I went into the front lobby, to my left and right were dozens of tables covered in white sheets with all this preachers tapes, cds, and books. He also did not live out a long life. He died early in a freak accident which I cannot mention as I do not want to give the clue that would reveal who he was. But again here's a man who was a pastor and traveling minister and God revealed something to me that could have been changed. I had no access to him and I only pray that others saw what I saw and were able to tell him. I also find it interesting that the preacher he quoted the most and actually copied in ministry, lived a full life.

We cannot accept the greed, the money changers, the business of the church, the world way of doing things, in the church. We need to warn those who preach this vain gospel and warn the sheep. Maybe this book is a type of sitting down to braid a whip and drive out the money changers.

We have all heard about the sheep in wolves clothing. They have wounded many. There are many walking wounded sheep outside the church walls. They will not come back to the mess we have created. But we need them as much as they need us. We are all part of a corporate body and all parts are in need of the other parts. Read John 17, where Jesus prayed we would all be one! Ephesians 4 says when we all come to a unity of the faith. That means us all, even those who are not of our opinion and doctrines, or those who are forsaking the fellowshipping of the saints. We must all be one! Not uniform in everyway, still individual members, but walking in love and unity.

One thing that aggravates me is the number of ministers who use the Word as a weapon against the sheep. You see the sword of the Spirit is not a weapon for sheep but for those we are in warfare against. It is for the principalities and rulers of darkness who have not received the message of defeat yet. We are not to be using the Word of the Spirit against fellow saints. Now the Word of God is good for reproof and correction, but not for those striving to be a child of God but for those in sin. I have met many leaders who use the Word as a weapon to manipulate others into what they want for them. The Word is to edify and build others up first and foremost, not to win battles about doctrine and theology or your latest greatest revelation against another saint. What's happened to keeping the unity of peace above all else? They are of the same family. This is why there are so many walking wounded. Friendly fire has taken them out. When people need help the most some religious freak just drives the knife deeper. Religion kills, relationship builds.

We need the walking wounded back in the church. We need pastors to wake up and preach the meat. We need the sheep to grow and become mature and become what God wants them to be. We as a body need to learn to Love. We need all parts of the body back in place and working together. That is the message of Ephesians Chapter 4. We need to be rooted and grounded in love building and edifying the sheep and then releasing them into their purpose and calling. In the least we need to pursue building mature believers who can follow God on their own. We need the Presence!

WHY ARE THE FISHERMEN EATING THE BAIT?

In war it is better for the enemy to wound a soldier than to kill him. It takes more resources and men to help that wounded soldier than a dead one. After a while the wounded, crying, screaming, in pain soldiers bog down the advancing army and they are forced to stop to treat them. It breaks the morale of the other soldiers to hear the screams and cries and have to stop to comfort them. It takes their eyes off the goal and the mission.

We can all argue about the prophetic, the faith folks, the money folks, the salvation folks, the worship folks, TV personalities, etc. But we are all one body. No group or church has it all figured out. No one has a corner on the market of God. No one has all the truth. We all know only in part. But together we as a complete body would be unstoppable. I know God has a remnant that has not bowed its heart to the idols and world system that has crept into the body of Christ.

What if we pulled away from the Catholic Church pyramid and instead of a single man at the top of our churches with "specialized knowledge" we bring in all five ministry gifts and served the people. How powerful would that be for the body to see the entire gifting's of God at work in a body, serving and building the body from the foundation up. As foundation of ministers with Jesus as the Chief cornerstone and lifting the body up towards God's. The current model which is just a few steps away from the Catholic, Plato, Nimrod pyramid. The one man at the top lording over the people is not a scriptural pattern, it is a worldly pattern and the space at the top is reserved for the antichrist not a man or a preacher. We must examine our methods, our motives and hold them up to the Word to determine how the body should be -- Not what conveniently works with in a dark and fallen world. Let's use the gifts God has in the body to support the body and develop the body to be all they can be. God does not need a man between us and Him with specialized knowledge or training. He already took care of that, and that was Jesus. He then told us that He would send the Holy Spirit to teach counsel and guide us. Many need to be taught how to hear the voice of the Spirit for themselves!

We must become again a priesthood that has the presence, not a form of it and we serve men as stewards, servants, love slaves of the King.

Jeremiah 3:3

3 Therefore the showers have been withholden, and there hath been no latter rain; and thou hadst a whore's forehead, thou refusedst to be ashamed.

Jeremiah 5:23

23 But this people hath a revolting and a rebellious heart; they are revolted and gone. 24 Neither say they in their heart, Let us now fear the Lord our God, that giveth rain, both the former and the latter, in his season: he reserveth unto us the appointed weeks of the harvest. 25 Your iniquities have turned away these things, and your sins have withholden good things from you.

Restoration of the Church

The topics, teachings and benefits of the church were hidden away from the church for many years. We often call that the dark ages. After Martin Luther the world began to change. The change began in the Church. Interestingly we call that era of history the reformation followed by the industrial revolution. When the Word of God was released by the Church it seems to have affected even the world. Luther helped start it and over the last 600 or so years many of the teachings of the early church have been restored to the church. God raised up different people through each generation to help bring back what had been hidden away for centuries. Martin Luther was "The just shall live by faith", then more followed him; down through history, until we get into the 1900's and the baptism of the Holy Spirit became prevalent. Then in the 1930's healing, then prophecy, discipleship, faith, teaching gifts, etc... Line upon line precept up on precept God restored His truth to the Church. Today there is a separate and grand set of prophecies that must be fulfilled. This is what the Prophet Hosea spoke about when he said,

Hosea 6
2 after two days will he revive us: in the third day he will raise us up, and we shall live in his sight. 3 Then shall we know, if we follow on to know the Lord: his going forth is prepared as the morning; and he shall come unto us as the rain, as the latter and former rain unto the earth.

From the day period (2nd day) that took place from 1000AD to

2000AD, God restored the truth to the corporate body of the Church through the raising up of individuals who took the spears and assault of their time. Each of those men and women raised the standard a little higher. Each paid a price for it. And yes many of those truths were taken to an extreme, and abused, but the truth of the Word stands. It seems as each truth had to go to an extreme to push it into every possible corner of the Church. Little by little they helped re-teach the Word of God to the Church. A restoring of the Word! The men and women we look to as heroes of the faith were fulfilling prophecy by being obedient to what God told them to do.

I see those men and women of great faith and anointing as signpost for something bigger and better coming. They opened our eyes to the possibilities in God. All of creation is waiting for the whole body of Christ to become the Sons of God. Those men and women showed us our potential in Christ.

He also stated that after the 2nd day, something would happen! Hosea says in the 3rd day, I will revive you so you may live in my presence. I do not see that as after the catching away of the saints, because in the next verse he says he will come to us as the rain, both latter and former rains. Why would He have to come to us as rain, if we were in heaven? There is an outpouring coming of such great magnitude that it will change the world. Rain is an outpouring of the Holy Spirit and that means marvelous miracles, signs and wonders. It means harvest. You have to have a spring rain to get the seed in the ground growing, but you also have to have a harvest rain to bring in the fruit later in the season. Spring rain and harvest rain --, as any farmer knows they're both necessary. Rain is coming, how do I know? Read Peter's passage that follows:

2 Peter 3:

8 but do not overlook this one fact, beloved, that with the Lord one day is as a thousand years, and a thousand years as one day. 9 The Lord is not slow to fulfill his promise as some count slowness, but is patient toward you, not wishing that any should perish, but that all should reach repentance. 10 But the day of the Lord will come like a thief, and then the heavens will pass away with a roar, and the heavenly bodies will be burned up and dissolved, and the earth and the works that are done on it will be exposed.

A day in the eyes of God is a thousand years. Well Hosea lived in the day before Jesus was on the earth. This would mean that the 3rd day from Adam had come and gone. And what prophet looks backwards? No they look forward to what is coming. So he has to be looking forward to the days after Jesus. Therefore he must be looking into the 3rd day since Jesus. That would be right about now, sometime after the year 2000AD. Rain is approaching, there is a storm on the horizon and the mighty wind is beginning to blow drops of rain on us. Get your barns ready for harvest! This is the last day. It all must happen in this day. We live in the day that all of creation has been waiting for with eager expectation!

I grew up in Oklahoma and you could see approaching wall clouds. You could feel that cool strong air blowing out ahead of the storm. Every once in a while the wind would carry a rain drop to us. Rain is coming and it is coming fast.

But one thing I see from this verse, it is a corporate body event. Those who have not bowed down to the god of money, the self built kingdoms, or the gods of the east. But a remnant that will allow God to be used for the purpose of Love, that none should perish. Young boys and girls in this upcoming generation can smell out the religious and they are not scared of anything. They can and will run further and faster than our generation. The world is waiting, even though it does not know it. It is approaching and it will be amazing but many will only watch because they would rather play the game of professional Christianity than pursue a relationship with God.

If you study Hosea, Joel and Zechariah, all three not only point out what is going to happen they give us a clue of how it will begin. The Azusa street revival did not happen by some mechanical time clock that God has. It happened because they acknowledged Him, they pressed in to Him, and they sought Him. They prayed and prayed and prayed more. They did not give up until they received from heaven what they knew was supposed to happen. Like Daniel they found the place where it was written and pursued it in prayer. We must, as each generation has before us, seek Him until we get it. Our relationship with Him must guide us and infect us.

Yeah! We live in the last day. The greatest day is the one where so much is going to happen. We get to be a part of it, if we want, if we choose. I believe that there is nothing written in the Word that God did not want in there for a reason. Have you ever wondered why each account of the transfiguration of Christ it says, "after the sixth day", another says "before the eight day" and one says "about seven days"?

I see something coming! Do you?

WORD & SPIRIT

We must be a Word and Spirit Church who is dependent on learning and being guided by His Word and Spirit. Eating the Bread of Life and drinking of the Spirit of Life. They are one in the same but also very different. Much like water that is frozen, water that is liquid, and water that is gas. It's all water. The Word is Jesus and the Spirit is the Holy Spirit and they are part of the Godhead. They are God but they also each serve a different purpose. We need both. We need the Word and the Spirit, both on the inside.

Jesus said eat this Bread. He called himself the Bread of Life. In John, the prophet called Him the Word. Jesus also said drink of this Spirit when He said, "Come to me all who thirst." We need the Holy Spirit the River of Life in us to activate the Word of Life in us. If we do both rivers of flowing water and Word will gush out of us. We will have all we need to minister to the World in need.

Jesus made a promise and said it is good for you that I go as I will send another to you. The Counselor, the Spirit of Truth, the Spirit of Love, the Holy Spirit and He will help you and be with you forever. He will be with you to always.

John 14

15 If ye love me, keep my commandments. 16 And I will pray the Father, and he shall give you another Comforter, that he may abide with you forever; 17 Even the Spirit of truth; whom the world cannot receive, because it seeth him not, neither knoweth him: but ye know him; for he dwelleth with you, and shall be in you. 18 I will not leave you comfortless: I will come to you. 19 Yet a little while, and the world seeth me no more;

but ye see me: because I live, ye shall live also. 20 At that day ye shall know that I am in my Father, and ye in me, and I in you. 21 He that hath my commandments, and keepeth them, he it is that loveth me: and he that loveth me shall be loved of my Father, and I will love him, and will manifest myself to him. 22 Judas saith unto him, not Iscariot, Lord, how is it that thou wilt manifest thyself unto us, and not unto the world? 23 Jesus answered and said unto him, If a man love me, he will keep my words: and my Father will love him, and we will come unto him, and make our abode with him. 24 He that loveth me not keepeth not my sayings: and the word which ye hear is not mine, but the Father's which sent me. 25 These things have I spoken unto you, being yet present with you. 26 But the Comforter, which is the Holy Ghost, whom the Father will send in my name, he shall teach you all things, and bring all things to your remembrance, whatsoever I have said unto

Jesus is telling us that once He goes He will send another to help us. That another is the Spirit of truth, the Third person of the Godhead, The Holy Spirit. Jesus is sitting at the right hand of the Father and He sent the Holy Spirit after sitting down to help us and be in us. That is what He means when He said, my Father and I will make our abode with Him. If you have the Holy Spirit you have God in you. We need to learn how to trust that which is in the inside of us.

If we trusted the Holy Spirit with our lives we would never want, never miss it, and never walk outside of love. We would act like the apostles did after the day of Pentecost and even our shadows would contain the virtue, the very substance of the Holy Spirit. We need the Holy Spirit and not just so we can speak in tongues of angels but to accomplish this mission. To walk in Love, to walk in power, to be the light we are called to be.

Jesus relied on the Holy Spirit and even said that He did nothing of Himself but only as He saw the Spirit do.

Isaiah even said in 11:3 that Jesus would do only as he hears of the Father

1 And there shall come forth a rod out of the stem of Jesse ,and a Branch shall grow out of his roots: 2 And the spirit of the Lord shall rest upon him, the spirit of wisdom and understanding, the spirit of counsel and might, the spirit of knowledge and of the fear of the Lord; 3 And

shall make him of quick understanding in the fear of the Lord: and he shall not judge after the sight of his eyes, neither reprove after the hearing of his ears:

Jesus said in John 5:19

19 Then answered Jesus and said unto them, Verily, verily, I say unto you, The Son can do nothing of himself, but what he seeth the Father do: for what things soever he doeth, these also doeth the Son likewise. 20 For the Father loveth the Son, and sheweth him all things that himself doeth: and he will shew him greater works than these, that ye may marvel.

Jesus then promised the Holy Spirit who would do the same.

John 16:13

13 Howbeit when he, the Spirit of truth, is come, he will guide you into all truth: for he shall not speak of himself; but whatsoever he shall hear, that shall he speak: and he will shew you things to come. 14 He shall glorify me: for he shall receive of mine, and shall shew it unto you.

If a prophet of old said Jesus would come and depend upon God for what He hears, says and does, and then Jesus Himself fulfilled it. Then He promised that the Holy Spirit Himself would do the same. He was totally dependent upon God for all He did and said. That is Jesus, totally dependent on God. He said that when the Holy Spirit came that the precious Holy Spirit would tell us the same way, the same manner. If Jesus, our crowning example and the wonderful Holy Spirit were both dependent on God and each other, how can we not be any less dependent on God?

We must learn to walk in total dependency upon God for all we are and do. We must teach others to do the same. I would rather teach others to be dependent on God than me any day! It requires so much commitment and prayer, more prayer and more prayer. We must be holy and clean. We cannot expect to be led if we are living in sin. We must be men and women of love and be rooted and grounded in this love. We must allow the Spirit of God, the Holy Spirit to lead us and teach us. In Acts it shows that the Holy Spirit will speak to us, guide us, compel us, tell us things to come and even be grieved by us. We must allow Him access to our hearts and then allow Him to teach us dependency on Him. We must trust, rely on and throw ourselves daily on Him. Jesus said, "My sheep know my voice." Earlier we spoke about obeying the voice of the Lord, (Deut 28) that is obeying the Holy Spirit. We need to learn how to follow Him in everything we do and say. We need to be totally dependent on Him. That is walking in the supernatural and Spirit led life.

We do that with the Partnership of the Holy Spirit. The Holy Spirit is our coach, our partner, our teacher, our guide and He knows it all. How can we expect to walk as He did, if we cannot depend on the Spirit like He did? We need the Spirit of God to do this. He will speak to us and teach us. He will navigate us through the Word and teach us. We need to know the Word and the Spirit.

We need the Word to build a foundation of Love and truth in us and we need to Spirit to bring it to life. We need both. One is as important as the other.

I often teach that the Word and the Spirit are like this.

As a drill instructor we had to teach privates land navigation armed only with a map and a compass. First we did hours of classroom teaching on maps explaining what each thing on a map was. Then we took them to the field and made them navigate to a set spot. Those who made it moved on to the next lesson. Next lesson was how to use a compass. We would teach them first and then take them to the field and leave them out there and pick them up at the desired destination. Then the final test was giving them a map and compass and using both to get to desired location. Using the map was easy to a degree, using the compass usually is where most privates, young newbie's, ran into problems. But if you gave them both a compass and map, usually they would arrive at the desired location faster and easier. You see the Word is the Map; the Bible is the instruction book that can show you how to navigate through. The Spirit is the compass and he can lead you in the right direction, even if you have no idea what's ahead. You will always know where true north is, Love. The Agape Love of God can never fail; God is a Spirit and He is Love, we can say, and that The Holy Spirit is the Holy Spirit of Love! The Word and the Spirit work together. Together they keep you on path of the narrow road and get you to your destination faster and often with less stopping and starting. We need both the Word and Spirit.

Psalms 119:
105 Thy word is a lamp unto my feet and a light unto my path...

WHY ARE THE FISHERMEN EATING THE BAIT?

Romans 8:

14 As many as are led by the Spirit of God they are the sons of God.

We need both.

Years ago when in Desert Storm I received a letter from my parents. In that letter they wrote so many things and one part included apologizing for things they had done as parents. It was an awesome letter, even though it was probably based on a thought that I was going to die! But I read that letter over and over and it comforted me in hard times and put me at ease to know my parents loved me. I took that letter into Iraq in my chest pocket (right against my Bible). That is like the Word of God. It's a love letter we can read it over and over and love it. But there's more!

Upon arriving home to Oklahoma after the war, I got out of the car and started to walk up to my parents' house. My mom comes flying out the door, wraps her arms around me and begins to cry in joy. My former military dad calmly walks out the door, down the steps and has one of those great smiles that only a son gets from his dad. He wrapped both my mom and I up in a great big hug, as he fought back tears. That was awesome! It meant just as much to me as the letter did but that is the Spirit. The Holy Spirit is not a letter, He is a personable being. The third part of the Godhead and He wants to wrap us up, come inside and be the best partner, un-forsaking friend and guide in this realm we could ever have. He activates the letter and makes it real. He activates the Word, agrees with it and gives it the virtue and substance to be powerful and real. He is the demonstration of Love that we need to not just be letter carriers. We need the Spirit because where He is Lord, there is freedom. He always agrees with the Word and is the voice of Love.

We need both...

Recently I had an experience that might help you. When I arrived in the country I am currently in, I was praying in the Spirit everyday. I was doing everything I could to follow Jude 20 & 21 which is to pray in the Spirit and stay in Love. We had side stepped many of the problems most missionaries and ex pats had moving to this country. I heard what others said about "how to do things" but never acknowledged it any more than a "thanks." I would go away and just let the Holy Spirit; my partner and coach to help me avoid those issues and then left that advice alone.

We seemed to walk right through so many things others had struggled through. I did not go around gloating and making public statements about it. It was just between me and Him.

Then I needed to go to the border to take care of the duty on my vehicle. I knew what I should have been expected to pay and I had it in my pocket. I made one very bad decision. Several folks had said, "Ok this is the way you have to do it here." I listened and did what they suggested I do. Other saints made these suggestions. I did them. I went to the border and they had no mercy, they attempted to charge me more in duty for my vehicle than I had paid for it in the US. No mercy. They would not budge. They ended up seizing my vehicle and my sons and I had to take a taxi back to town. Later the next morning when I woke up the Holy Spirit addressed me on this. I saw what I had done, I had stepped out of love but more importantly I took the advice of someone other than the Lord. I repented and He sent someone to me that next day to help. I still paid way too much but less than they originally demanded and I ended up having to borrow the money to get it out of customs.

I knew I needed to listen to Him and not others. Everything we had done to this point was by the leading of the Holy Spirit or staying in Love. I taught this right away in the class that week. I learned the hard way. We need to become so convinced of His love for us and that he will lead us that we refuse to let anything get in between the connection we have with Him. I teach others, that above all else protect that personal vital living contact with the Holy Spirit. I stepped out of that love relationship by not listening to Him when I knew He was speaking. I listened to the wrong leading. Stay in Love at all cost. That is the place of integrity, supernatural leadership, miracles and everything the World needs.

We often don't get it right every time, He is a forgiving God and He wants the best for us. We have to be dependent on Him and not on how others do it. We have for years helped others plant churches in many countries. Always the pattern was, get a group and grow into a building. Then God directed us to our current assignment. He led me to the building first, without a single person other than my family to fellowship, but over and over people showed up and cried as they stepped into the building and realized what God was doing. It is worth being led more than being practical. Even though for years we had done it the other way, The Holy Spirit had a different plan this time!

WHY ARE THE FISHERMEN EATING THE BAIT?

The Word is truth and gives us a basis for all things pertaining to life and godliness, the Holy Spirit is our coach who as Jesus said, will show you things to come. He is here to guide us and help us understand what the Word says and how to navigate this world. We have to have both.

We need to meditate day and night on the Word and communion with the Holy Spirit. I love what is says in Psalm 1, to delight in the Lord, meditate day and night. Bind it to your heart. When we delight in the Word and The Spirit we have a joy and enjoyment of both that makes life so grand. I do all I can to protect that time and relationship with Him. I did not become all this overnight, it was a relationship that has grown over the years. Just like my wife and I, I still learn from her and enjoy her company and would you believe that once I turned that TV off, I found more time for both God and my wife!

I Love the story about King David as he was bringing the Ark of the Covenant back to the temple. He danced in front of it as he went along. He was excited and full of joy! He knew that having the Presence of the Living God was going to change things and cause them to be overtaken with all the benefits of that relationship. He was excited and acting a fool because he knew what was about to happen. You see the presence of God, the Holy Spirit brings with Him all the benefits so many people have been in pursuit of, and the principles of God work for anyone who employee them, but the Presence and the company of the Holy Spirit, brings great joy and blessing.

I have taught on the Old Tabernacle, here is the Glory of God at the Mercy seat. That Glory provides the only light that there was in the Holy Of Holies. No artificial man made light in there, just the Presence and purity of God as the Glory. It was an experience, not just knowledge. They say that when the high priest, once a year, poured the blood on the mercy seat at Passover, that the Glory of God would come down and like a tornado of rushing wind; on Pentecost, descend on the Mercy seat and burn up the blood. God consumed the Blood of the sacrifice. It sounds like that day of Pentecost in Acts 2:4 when the Spirit fell and the fire separated on them. Now that Presence and Glory resides in new tabernacles. HE RESIDES IN US! The same powerful, presence that when someone touched Jesus, He said "I felt virtue, power go out of me". The presence of the Holy Spirit is not some mist or cloud; He is a substance that is more real than flesh and bone. The presence of God that once dwelt only in the Holy of Holies on the Mercy Seat dwells in us, if we allow it. The same presence that made David dance afoot dwells in me and you!

That presence missing is what made the people of Israel returning to the land after the 70 years of captivity cry out that

Haggai 2:
3 Who is left among you that saw this house in her first glory? And how do ye see it now? Is it not in your eyes in comparison of it as nothing?

They had seen the old temple and now the new one was missing something! Haggai goes on to say, the Glory of the latter house is supposed to be greater than the latter. But the people wailed and called it as nothing! The presence was not there. Why? Because the Ark was not there. The Ark was the resting place of God's presence. It was not there as it had been hidden to protect it from the invasion 70 years earlier. Therefore the temple was missing something. The returning Jews called it nothing. By the time Jesus walked the Earth, the Jews had a dead powerless religion, because they lacked the Presence of God. Much like today. Unfortunately entire generations of Gods people have missed or not experienced the true Presence and therefore they have no standard from which to teach it.

Growing Up Into Maturity

I am convinced that the new move of revival about to sweep the world will not be single individuals doing what many did during the Voice of Healing days or the days of one anointed man. It will be individual as well as a corporate movement. A unified remnant of diverse young and old, men and women who are not stuck in traditions of men. We have to teach them how to become what God wants, not what we preachers want or denominations want. God's love for them and the lost is more important than our opinions and doctrines of men.

We have to help bring them into maturity as sons and daughters.

1 Corinthians 13

1 Though I speak with the tongues of men and of angels, and have not charity, I am become as sounding brass, or a tinkling cymbal. 2 And though I have the gift of prophecy, and understand all mysteries, and all knowledge; and though I have all faith, so that I could remove mountains, and have not charity, I am nothing. 3 And though I bestow all my goods to feed the poor, and though I give my body to be burned, and have not charity, it profiteth me nothing.

4 Charity suffereth long, and is kind; charity envieth not; charity vaunteth not itself, is not puffed up, 5 Doth not behave itself unseemly, seeketh not her own, is not easily provoked, thinketh no evil; 6 Rejoiceth not in iniquity, but rejoiceth in the truth; 7 Beareth all things, believeth all things, hopeth all things, endureth all things.

8 Charity never faileth: but whether there be prophecies, they

shall fail; whether there be tongues, they shall cease; whether there be knowledge, it shall vanish away. 9 For we know in part, and we prophesy in part. 10 But when that which is perfect is come, then that which is in part shall be done away.

11 When I was a child, I spake as a child, I understood as a child, I thought as a child: but when I became a man, I put away childish things. 12 For now we see through a glass, darkly; but then face to face: now I know in part; but then shall I know even as also I am known.

13 And now abideth faith, hope, charity, these three; but the greatest of these is charity.

Chapter 14
1 Follow after charity, and desire spiritual gifts, but rather that ye may prophesy.

I love how Paul is dropping hints here about when perfection comes, when Love comes, the rest is of naught. Do you also catch the hint here he is giving us? That Love is not about being a child. You see that the Love he speaks of here is not just being kind, or friendly. It is the God kind of love. The love that walks in and says, "There you are!" It is the kind of love that never gives up, never surrenders, never attacks, never turns its back. It is the love that cannot fail. It is the God kind of Love. The God kind of love makes it our duty to love our enemies and to love those who hurt us, and to love those who abuse us.

Paul tells us that when love comes that the imperfect disappears. Love is the perfection we seek. Love cannot fail. Everything else can. Everything else will disappear but Love remains. We included the first verse of chapter 14 as well. It carries this thought: to pursue, to eagerly desire, as in make it your greatest quest to follow after love. It alone will satisfy the desires of your heart. It is the Spirit and it is God.

Years ago I was in a position where I had been done very wrong. It actually cost us all we had. We lost everything all due to jealousy. I had found out who had been used by the devil in this vicious attack. I wanted to expose them and let everyone know what had happened. As I prayed on the matter; not always being polite with my words, God said "My love for them outweighs your opinion of them." O my! I knew God was right and I had to walk in Love. I kept silent and moved on, putting it behind me. It was hard and I am sure I was not perfect in how I handled it but thank God for His Mercy and Love. Today years later, I see that if I had gone after this man in court or in the Church, today I would have lost out. And because I did follow after love, with in a year I was able to bless that man in a different way and he received it. Jesus said they that Love me obey me. We must obey his commands if we Love Him. No matter the pain or whatever else may happen. What we think about other people is not important. God loves them more than your opinion of them. I was used to lift that man up later because I listened to the Spirit of God and did not do what I had an earthly right to do. My rights are overruled by the Love of God.

John tells us in 1 John that God is Love. If you study the entire Word of God you will find four things that cannot fail: God, His mercy, the Word and Love. God is all of those things. He is Mercy. He is Love. He is Word & Spirit. If we want to worship Him we must do so in Spirit and Truth. If God is also Truth and Love so then it sounds like to worship God and to Love God is to get into this Love, the unfailing love. This is the only relationship that will satisfy, teach you, coach you, protect you, provide for you.... Sounds like a father doesn't it?

Ephesians 2:

14 For this cause I bow my knees unto the Father of our Lord Jesus Christ, 15 Of whom the whole family in heaven and earth is named, 16 That he would grant you, according to the riches of his glory, to be strengthened with might by his Spirit in the inner man; 17 That Christ may dwell in your hearts by faith; that ye, being rooted and grounded in love, 18 May be able to comprehend with all saints what is the breadth, and length, and depth, and height; 19 And to know the love of Christ, which passeth knowledge, that ye might be filled with all the fullness of God. 20 Now unto him that is able to do exceeding abundantly above all that we ask or think, according to the power that worketh in us, 21 Unto him be glory in the church by Christ Jesus throughout all ages, world without end. Amen.

We must follow after love with all we have within us. We will find that the Holy Spirit who is also God is also Love. If we follow after love we will do as it says in Ephesians, Paul said that you may be rooted and grounded in love... Established in Love, our foundation is to be in love. This love that can never fail... How great is that... I am convinced that the cures of the sickness of the world can be satisfied if the Church would pursue this unfailing love. This unfailing Spirit, this unfailing God, in an unfailing relationship.

He also says that we may comprehend this Love of Christ, the Love of God. We need it by His Spirit in our inner man. Then He speaks of being filled with all the fullness of God. Oh My. I want that! I want to be rooted and grounded in Love that I may be able to be full to the Fullness of God! Then no longer swayed back and forth by cunning teaching of men! I want that for every believer and I preach that with a passion. It's it time to grow up and become all He wants for us.

We cannot control God, we cannot control His mercy, but we can choose to walk or practice this Love. Romans 5:8, says that this love was shed abroad in our hearts. It's there my friend. Study it and begin to practice it. As you do it will grow within you. As you meditate on Love and what it is, you will go deeper and further than you could otherwise. You see if Love is our foundation, the best foundation, then we can build further, higher and faster and reach further with that strong, unfailing foundation. Go for it and see what happens. Follow after Love; follow after the path of Jesus. It cannot fail us.

Many people love to talk about how Jesus made a whip and drove the money changers out and even rebuked the "vipers". Please understand, He did this with the backing of LOVE. He first had, possessed acquired, and maintained this relational Love walk. Yes He was rebuking them but He was also rooted and ground in love first. He spent more time healing and loving then He did rebuking. Don't get off into correcting everyone else, let's take the plank out of our own eyes and root ourselves in love. If you can't do it in Love don't try. The voice of The Spirit is always a voice of Love.

Matthew 6:

33 But seek ye first the kingdom of God, and his righteousness; and all these things shall be added unto you.

For many years we have been preaching the benefits of being saved. We have produced a system that produces people after something instead of Someone. Many people want the riches and wisdom of Solomon, but they are getting the cart before the horse. Go back and study all recorded accounts of when God came to King Solomon, he was at the alter praying... He was seeking that relationship. He was in pursuit of God. He was living out what King David had charged him with...Love God with all your heart, all you soul and all your strength. Love God with all you are my friend, love Him with everything that you possess and have obtained, run towards Him with your daily actions and commitments. Go for it. Then see if God doesn't also show up in your closet and say to you what He said to Solomon. Love is the answer. It is the path of righteousness and the path of never failing. Let's make right judgments and stop these vain pursuits and activities that prevent us from knowing Him.

Jesus said that some would come to Him and say" Did we not do wonders in your name" Many will think they have their tickets punched to the throne of God but, do we? Jesus used the word Know. That word means to know as in an intimate way, like a husband and wife. My wife and I became one flesh, so must you with God, Jesus, and the Holy Spirit.

John 17

1 These words spake Jesus, and lifted up his eyes to heaven, and said, Father, the hour is come; glorify thy Son, that thy Son also may glorify thee:2 As thou hast given him power over all flesh, that he should give eternal life to as many as thou hast given him. 3 And this is life eternal, that they might know thee the only true God, and Jesus Christ, whom thou hast sent. 4 I have glorified thee on the earth: I have finished the work which thou gavest me to do. 5 And now, O Father, glorify thou me with thine own self with the glory which I had with thee before the world was. 6 I have manifested thy name unto the men which thou gavest me out of the world: thine they were, and thou gavest them me; and they have kept thy word. 7 Now they have known that all things whatsoever thou hast given me are of thee. 8 For I have given unto them the words which thou gavest me; and they have received them, and have known surely that I came out from thee, and they have believed that thou didst send me. 9 I pray for them: I pray not for the world, but for them which thou hast given me; for they are thine. 10 And all mine are thine, and thine are mine; and I am glorified in them. 11 And now I am no more in the world, but these are in the world, and I come to thee. Holy Father,

keep through thine own name those whom thou hast given me, that they may be one, as we are. 12 While I was with them in the world, I kept them in thy name: those that thou gavest me I have kept, and none of them is lost, but the son of perdition; that the scripture might be fulfilled. 13 13 And now come I to thee; and these things I speak in the world, that they might have my joy fulfilled in themselves. 14 I have given them thy word; and the world hath hated them, because they are not of the world, even as I am not of the world. 15 I pray not that thou shouldest take them out of the world, but that thou shouldest keep them from the evil. 16 They are not of the world, even as I am not of the world. 17 Sanctify them through thy truth: thy word is truth. 18 As thou hast sent me into the world, even so have I also sent them into the world. 19 And for their sakes I sanctify myself, that they also might be sanctified through the truth. 20 Neither pray I for these alone, but for them also which shall believe on me through their word; 21 That they all may be one; as thou, Father, art in me, and I in thee, that they also may be one in us: that the world may believe that thou hast sent me. 22 And the glory which thou gavest me I have given them; that they may be one, even as we are one:23 I in them, and thou in me, that they may be made perfect in one; and that the world may know that thou hast sent me, and hast loved them, as thou hast loved me. 24 Father, I will that they also, whom thou hast given me, be with me where I am; that they may behold my glory, which thou hast given me: for thou lovedst me before the foundation of the world. 25 O righteous Father, the world hath not known thee: but I have known thee, and these have known that thou hast sent me. 26 And I have declared unto them thy name, and will declare it: that the love wherewith thou hast loved me may be in them, and I in them.

Jesus prayed in John 17, that we would be one, "even as you and I are one". He wants you to be one with Him. He wants you to share, experience and obtain the same Glory He had on this earth. He wants the Church as a corporate body to be one. We cannot accomplish what God has given us to do by being one here and one there. We must purify ourselves and become one with Him and one as a corporate body. I believe it will happen before the end. God is bringing many sons to glory and He will see it happen. I intend to be a part and will follow after the way of unfailing love and stay in that. Jesus is coming for one bride, not several different ones. We must be without spot or wrinkle and that only happens through love.

God is coming for a bride. If as husbands our wife came walking down the aisle disheveled, dirty, with messed up hair and such would we as her love be happy? All this time to get yourself perfect, ready and you come out looking like you just got out of a fight? But that is exactly how the bride is right now. Our factions and separations of minor issues have kept us from being ready for the wedding.

Galatians 5:
6 For in Jesus Christ neither circumcision availeth anything, nor uncircumcision; but faith which worketh by love.

One version says,"the only thing that matters is faith expressing itself through love." Such a good nugget.

Galatians 5:
14 For all the law is fulfilled in one word, even in this; Thou shalt love thy neighbor as thyself. 15 But if ye bite and devour one another, take heed that ye be not consumed one of another.

Everything can be summed up in this one command. Love. I appreciate the verse 15 as well, it is part of the reason it took me 16 years to write this book. I cannot do it just to criticize and harm people but my heart is that you see the sign post and move in the right direction.

Galatians 5:
16 This I say then, Walk in the Spirit, and ye shall not fulfill the lust of the flesh.

Walk in the Spirit, which is awesome. That Spirit is Love. You cannot separate Love from God nor can you separate it from the Holy Spirit. Walk in the Spirit you will walk in Love. You will grow into maturity. Becoming the Fullness of Christ in this earth.

Have you ever taken the time to notice that the fruit of the Spirit in Galatians 5:22 is so similar to the description to the description of Love in 1 Corinthians 13: 4-8

Galatians 5:

22 But the fruit of the Spirit is love, joy, peace, longsuffering, gentleness, goodness, faith, 23 Meekness, temperance: against such there is no law. 24 And they that are Christ's have crucified the flesh with the affections and lusts. 25 If we live in the Spirit, let us also walk in the Spirit.

I Corinthians 13

4 Charity suffereth long, and is kind; charity envieth not; charity vaunteth not itself, is not puffed up, 5 Doth not behave itself unseemly, seeketh not her own, is not easily provoked, thinketh no evil; 6 Rejoiceth not in iniquity, but rejoiceth in the truth; 7 Beareth all things, believeth all things, hopeth all things, endureth all things.

8 Charity never faileth:

Now you might be at a point where you think I got off on a rabbit trail here. But don't you see the Love in this? Can't you see that Love. Only that Love, that type of Glory will satisfy your heart. For years we have been in pursuit of Glory, anointing, prosperity, faith, etc... All things those are truth benefits of the sons of God. But they are not the most excellent way. Those things had to be restored to the Church as prophesied in Hosea 6:2 but they are teaching about the relational benefits of knowing God. Not God. You can tell anyone about me and what I look like and what I'm doing but that does not mean we know each other. Only a relationship produced that kind of love.

Hosea 6:2 part two says that we will live in His presence, but further down in verse He says let us acknowledge Him. Press into Him. Then He will send the rains. That is in this earth, this time. He wants to be in us and have us live in His presence now! In the Third day! Not in the sweet by and by, but now! We should as Jesus, said to abide in Him and He and the Father will dwell in us. If we have the Father, Jesus, and the Holy Spirit truly in us, He will take care of His house. You. You are the Temple of God now. He will care for that house and meet the needs of that house. We don't need to resort to games and business practices that the world uses to meet our needs. He wants to meet our need and give us power to do the job. He wants to fill us and let us do the greater works. It is time to get our eyes off the things that are not happening and agreeing to the lack of power and love. It is time to acknowledge it and press into it and strive for it. A revival is coming and the Bride will leave afterwards, are you ready or will you be too busy maintaining and murmuring. Get up and lift your eyes to the standard set before you and get in His presence. He alone will satisfy the cry of our hearts. His presence, the presence of love, the presence of truth. The virtue and substance of God. The substance of Love.

I am convinced that Love it the cure for all that ails us. If we love and pursue Him we will succeed. We will press in and acknowledge Him. He will come to us as the latter rain. Jesus said HE and the Father would dwell in us! He will make his home in us.

You see it is all about a love relationship with the father. Compared to marriage by Paul. Does your wife love you now after all these years of marriage out of a duty, or a where else can I go? That is not love. Are you kind to your wife? Are you kind with God. What Kind with God? Yes kind with God. Your wife wants you to be kind to her, how is God any different. If it were not so then how can we ever grieve the Holy Spirit? How can we humans have emotions and be created in His image and He not have emotions. God wants to be married to you and love you and He demands that love in return. If it was not so then why was the first command to Love God with all your heart, all your soul and all your strength? Why did Jesus re instate that first law of love in John 13:34?

You see God uses the comparisons on marriage in the Word for a reason. You must become one flesh with her and Him. Give Him what you gave your wife. With all your heart and all your strength.

Where Are The Fisherman

Matthew 4:19
" And he saith unto them, Follow me, and I will make you fishers of men. 20 And they straightway left their nets, and followed him."

Mark 1:17
"And Jesus said unto them, Come ye after me, and I will make you to become fishers of men. 18 And straightway they forsook their nets, and followed him."

Fisherman should be in the water or boat casting nets and bait to catch the fish, not hanging out on shore watching others fish. Idle fisherman lead to idleness and all sorts of ungodly things.

A true fisherman is a Goer, one who gets out into the water, not sitting on the shore watching. If you're a carpenter and you tell people you're a carpenter then I would expect you can show me something you have built. If you're a fisherman show me your catch. Teach others how to fish. There are those who sit on shore and fix nets, meals and other logistic items. If you cannot fish, send someone.

Jesus said he would make us fishers of men, meaning He would teach us, supply us and then release us to go be actual fishers of men.

Let us look into this a little, let us first discover what we look like in the spirit realm. I am convinced that the best interpreter of scripture is scripture so let us examine a few texts before we go into the prophetic.

WHY ARE THE FISHERMEN EATING THE BAIT?

Mark 8:22

22 And he cometh to Bethsaida; and they bring a blind man unto him, and besought him to touch him. 23 And he took the blind man by the hand, and led him out of the town; and when he had spit on his eyes, and put his hands upon him, he asked him if he saw ought. 24 And he looked up, and said, I see men as trees, walking. 25 After that he put his hands again upon his eyes, and made him look up: and he was restored, and saw every man clearly.

It is interesting that in this passage the blind man's eyes were opened, but something was wrong -- or was it? First Jesus opened his Spiritual eyes, then the man said he saw the trees walking around as if men. Well I have been witness to many miracles and one thing always happens, the people with you move into a position to be able to see the miracle happen. The disciples probably were standing behind Jesus looking at the blind man. Who do you think that the man saw? Note that Jesus led him out of town. He got him out away from everyone else, just the disciples were there. The disciples were there walking around. And thus we can learn from this that we children of God can be referred to as trees in the Word of God.

Let's look at another to be sure

Rev 9: 4

And it was commanded them that they should not hurt the grass of the earth, neither any green thing, neither any tree; but only those men which have not the seal of God in their foreheads.

So trees are men! Now let's read a great look into the future!

Ezekiel 47

1 Afterward he brought me again unto the door of the house; and, behold, waters (streams from the temple, water meaning Spirit) issued out from under the threshold of the house eastward: for the forefront of the house stood toward the east, and the waters came down from under from the right side of the house, at the south side of the altar. 2 Then brought he me out of the way of the gate northward, and led me about the way without unto the utter gate by the way that looketh eastward; and, behold, there ran out waters (2nd stream meaning the

BROTHER JOHN

Word proceeding from the temple, presence of God) on the right side. (THERE ARE TWO DIFFERENT RIVERS THAT BECOME ONE! SOME CALL THESES THE RIVERS OF THE WORD AND THE SPIRIT Reference Psalm 23, rod and staff also means word and spirit) 3 And when the man that had the line in his hand went forth eastward, he measured a thousand cubits (1 DAY), and he brought me through the waters; the waters were to the ankles. 4 Again he measured a thousand (2nd DAY), and brought me through the waters; the waters were to the knees. Again he measured a thousand (3rd Day), and brought me through; the waters were to the loins. 5 Afterward he measured a thousand (4th day) (this confused me at first as that would mean that the forth day was actually four days since Adam. Or is it that it is four days out from when Ezekiel lived? He lived in the day or the thousand year period before Jesus. Meaning he lived four days ago); and it was a river that I could not pass over: for the waters were risen, waters to swim in, a river that could not be passed over. 6 And he said unto me, Son of man, hast thou seen this? Then he brought me, and caused me to return to the brink of the river. 7 Now when I had returned, behold, (NOW HE SEES) at the bank of the river were very many trees (STUDY MARK 8:22-25 and Rev 9:4, trees are children of God, not just men but born again men) on the one side and on the other. 8 Then said he unto me, These waters issue out toward the east country, and go down into the desert, and go into the sea: (sea, the world of humanity) which being brought forth into the sea, the waters shall be healed. 9 And it shall come to pass, that everything that liveth, which moveth, whithersoever the rivers shall come, shall live (everywhere the water which is the Holy Spirit lives moves and has it freedom, living creatures live 2 Corinthians 3:17):and there shall be a very great multitude of fish (nations and nations of many different kinds of people), because these waters shall come thither: for they shall be healed; and every thing (we shall live by the river, as in Number 24:6-7, Jer 17:7-8) shall live whither the river cometh. 10 And it shall come to pass, that the fishers shall stand upon it from Engedi even unto Eneglaim (a quick search of these places reveals that they are desolate places, places people do not want to go to); they shall be a place to spread forth nets; (when we do crusades, we always cast and bring in the net) their fish shall be according to their kinds (all races all people), as the fish of the great sea, exceeding many (Multitudes, multitudes in the valley of decision

WHY ARE THE FISHERMEN EATING THE BAIT?

-Joel 3:14 & Rev 14:14-20). 11 But the miry places thereof and the marshes thereof shall not be healed; they shall be given to salt (2 peter 3:8 and more). 12 And by the river upon the bank thereof, on this side and on that side, shall grow all trees for meat, whose leaf shall not fade, neither shall the fruit (fruit of Spirit is Love, love cannot fail) thereof be consumed: it shall bring forth new fruit according to his months (also says always in season in NIV), because their waters they issued out of the sanctuary (from the presence of God!) :and the fruit thereof shall be for meat (life and living, the meat of the Word is Love), and the leaf thereof for medicine (healing).

Ezekiel lived four days ago; He was looking forward at an event to come. He sees the springs (Hebrew word used in the plural means spring that becomes a flood) coming from the temple, which there are two, they become one, The Word and the Spirit. As they become one they increase as they progress in time forward. Even Jesus said, "You shall see greater works." Ezekiel is seeing into the prophetic future here, he would not refer to the day Jesus walked as day four or from what has already happened in past, so it must be from his time forward, the 4th day (specific to this vision) being the time of the greater and latter rain. After the year 2000 the fourth day into the future. And it is an outpouring, a flood, river that no man can cross. An outpouring that will cause multitudes to come into the valley of decision and the fruit of those fishermen will never fail (love) and they will have healing power. You see this goes hand in hand with the end time vision of Joel, Hosea and even Isaiah about the last days. Also in Zechariah the day of the later rain. The outpouring of His Spirit is for the harvest of the earth, it is for the lost. But someone must go be a fisherman and cast the nets and bring the fish to the feet, the banks of the river, the Church so they can be healed and fed. Some versions of Bible say that the fruit will be in season at all times.

Ezekiel is telling us a different version of what many other prophets have told us.

Jeremiah 17

7 Blessed is the man who trusts in the Lord, whose trust is the Lord. 8 He is like a tree planted by water, that sends out its roots by the stream, and does not fear when heat comes, for its leaves remain green, and is not anxious in the year of drought, for it does not cease to bear fruit

BROTHER JOHN

I want to preach the Gospel and for the fruit of Love to never cease, to never fail! If I'm a tree then I want my leaves of healing to remain green. Paul said to eagerly desire spiritual gifts.

Romans 10:
14 How then shall they call on him in whom they have not believed? And how shall they believe in him of whom they have not heard? And how shall they hear without a preacher? 15 And how shall they preach, except they be sent? As it is written, How beautiful are the feet of them that preach the gospel of peace, and bring glad tidings of good things!

They must hear and according to Ezekiel there are places for spreading nets, specific places for doing crusades. Fishermen spread nets. It says from En Elgam to En Gedhi, those are desolate places that now one goes to anymore. We have to be willing to go to the hard places and the desolate places to preach to them. We have to be willing to weigh the cost and go just to reach the one.

It goes on to say that the fishermen bring the catch to the banks of the river. The church is on the banks of the river. The trees! The fruit trees are there, waiting to give Love and healing. Waiting to give life and healing to all who come. They will be many types and kinds of people and all sorts of shapes and sizes, they will have all kinds of issues, but we must care for them, feed them and Love them. We must shepherd them!

We are the trees and the same sap that flows through Jesus can flow though us. Remember the teaching Jesus did "I am the vine you are the branch" We are grafted in and we share in the benefits of that blood. We produce the fruit, not the vine, the branches produce the fruit. The same sap that flows through Jesus the vine flows through us when we stay connected with Him. We must keep that vital living contact with the Spirit. We the branches are the only part of the tree producing leaves and fruit. Get plugged in and allow Him to dwell in you so that the rivers of flowing water may gush out of you. The world needs it and is like we before we met Him, they don't even realize their great need. But we do.

Jesus Himself stated "Follow me I will make you fishers of men". The fishermen have a job to do and they bring the multitudes into the Church to be fed, matured and sent back out. Today like in the days Jesus walked on the earth, the gifts and the equipment supplied to us for the job of fishing have been misdirected and used to support a Levitical like priesthood that is robbing God. God called the priesthood out in Malachi

Malachi 2:
7 For the priest's lips should keep knowledge, and they should seek the law at his mouth: for he is the messenger of the Lord of hosts. 8 But ye are departed out of the way; ye have caused many to stumble at the law; ye have corrupted the covenant of Levi, saith the Lord of hosts. 9 Therefore have I also made you contemptible and base before all the people, according as ye have not kept my ways, but have been partial in the law.

The fishermen are eating the bait intended to feed the flock and bring in the harvest!

Many have taught that this chapter in Ezekiel is a picture of revival and I agree, It will take the Word and the Spirit, flowing together to become a flood that no man can cross, meaning not a man made program, system, method, it will be God and God alone. God had to rescue him from the river and bring him to the bank of the river. There we see the Church. Multitudes in the valley of decision and we are going to see it.

When those nations of people are brought to the banks of the river, they should be experiencing the best of us... which is of course God himself, His presence not ours! There is a key to developing that..

LOVE IS THE KEY TO THE KINGDOM

The word love and its variations are used over 573 times in the Bible, including Loved, loveth, lovest

Love as used in the original text, specifically in NT is broken down into two primary words Agape and Phileo. Between the two of them there are 8 words that side with either the man kind of love or the God kind of love. Phileo is man and Agape is God kind of love. Agape is used 126 times and was first introduced by Jesus in Mat 5:43. The other main word for the God kind of love is Agapao and it was used 86 times and first introduced in Mt 24:12 when He said the love of many would grow cold.

DEFINED
PHILEO LOVE

Phileo is brotherly love. Brother or sisterly love. Love of the brethren, brotherly kindness. To be fond of. In Greek meaning friend or affectionate duty. Also rooted in

Philandanos fond of man
Philotekios maternal love
Philadelpis to love brethren
Philidelphia brotherly love

Study the following verses concerning Phileo love 1 Th 4:9, 1 Pt 1:22, Rom 12:10, Heb 13:1, 2 Pt 1:7, 1 TH 4:9

THELEMA to have an inclination or determination for, a habit
Agape
In Greek is rooted in Agapao both meaning the God kind of love.

WHY ARE THE FISHERMEN EATING THE BAIT?

Agape is like a love feast, a love that sees others and celebrates, gives, rejoices and proclaims its passionate desire for the object of love. It protects, feeds, cares for mends, sorrows for... It is what Jesus said two times to Peter when restoring him, and then changed to Phileo on the third question, before Peter got the hint. Agape is also used as a noun in some parts of the Word. Agape is the noun used to indicate the person and presence of God the Father Himself.

Agapao is a social or moral love that focuses on how we see, treat and deal with others, still rooted in the God kind of love. Meaning in our treatment of others, it has behind it a root Greek word, AGAB which gives the meaning to breathe to inhale this passion, this love. As well as EGEB in Hebrew (not Greek) which gives meaning to an active animated descriptive, energetic word to much love or very lovely. It is a wild and exciting love that, much like King David when he danced before the Ark of the Covenant. The presence of God was with Him and he made a fool of himself! This Greek word is often used as an adverb in the Word.

Basically the two words give us an active, living, breathing, substantial, essence of love that, almost a moment by moment breathing of God himself. Love is a virtue, a substance, just like God. A love feast. A party like with a wedding, a celebration set apart just for you. With Him your bridegroom! I hear people say all the time, Love is an adverb. Yes but it is also a noun and pronoun. Love is not an information packet, it is a being. It is God, It is the Holy Spirit. Just because we define Love in an informational way here, please do not forget we are speaking of Him.

Old Testament words for love

AHAB to have affection for, used 74 times like Gen 27:4

AHABAH is Female love for, affection for used 31 times as in Gen 29:30, it is female version of AHAB

CHASATIAG is to love, to delight in , to desire to long for, to pursue (As in God's love) used in Psalm 97:10 and Duet 7:7 only twice in Old Testament

AGABAH means to hold inordinate affection for. Meaning you place something above truth or real love. For instance a preacher who preaches the word incorrectly and you accept it in the name of love. That is actually inordinate affection. You love man more than God.

Paul said in 1 Corinthians 14:1 "FOLLOW AFTER THE WAY OF LOVE" Pursue this love with all you have, make it your greatest quest and passion in life. Desire it and focus on it. Set your eye on it. As you will see it is the most excellent way! Galatians 5:6 states that the only thing that matters it is faith expressing itself through love!

This Scripture is often quoted on our radio show, "Love never fails" because it holds so much meaning. What are we pursuing? We love to preach about Paul being a love slave and how committed he was, but we can be the same. Paul knew that Love was the only way. The Word of God is His love letter to us. We need to read it understanding that it is God's long and time consuming explanation of His love for us and not just a bunch of rules and regulations. We have to understand that each and every one of us relates to God differently and the Word of God addresses each and every possible avenue of love that is needed for all of us individuals. He had all of humanity in mind when He wrote this letter. Not just me and how I think, but all people.

If we follow after love we will love God (Dt 6:5, 10:12, 11:1, Mt 22:3) We will love our neighbors (Lev 19:18, Mat 22:39) We will love strangers (Dt 10:19.) We will love Wisdom (Proverbs 4:6) we will love good (Amos 5:15) we will love mercy (Micah 6:8) We will love truth (Zechariah 8:19), we will love our enemies (Mt 5:44, Lk 6:27) We will love one another, (John 123:34) We will love God's name (Ps 69:36, Ps 11:9, Ps 13:2) as well as God's Word (Ps 119:113&119&127)

If we pursue love as Paul said we should, we will love with all our heart, soul and strength (Mt 22:37, Luke 10:27) you will love others as you love yourself (Mt 22:39), You will love exceedingly (Ps 119:167) you will love even as Christ loved us (John 15:12) If we love we will love enough to lay down our lives for each other (John 15:13) If we pursue love we will do so without hypocrisy (Romans 12:9) When we pursue love we will do so by the Holy Spirit (2 Corinthians 6:6) We will pursue love in sincerity (2 Corinthians 8:8) As those who follow after love we will prove it in service to one another (Gal 5:13) also in forbearing one another (Eph 4:2). If we truly pursue and follow after love we will do so with a pure heart fervently (1 Peter22) we will prove it not in word but in Deed (1 John 3:18) and we will do it all with our fear as perfect Love (agape love) drives out fear! (1 John 4:18)

In Galatians 5:6, Paul said faith works by love. If your confession of faith is not working, check your love walk. If you're seemingly doing everything right and nothing is working, check your love walk. How are you treating God? How are you treating others? How are you treating yourself?

If you love, you will build others up. Love does not puff up or tear down others (unlike knowledge and doctrine), as it can only be constructive and edifying. True love pursues others and gives just as He sent His Son to do the same. If you love you will build people, even those who may not see eye to eye with you. Love always believes the best and treats them accordingly. We never provide a stumbling block. Bite that fleshy tongue and learn to keep your opinions to yourself and love them in the Love of God.

Jude also said, in Verse 21 and 22
21 Pray in the Spirit and build yourself up in your faith 22 AND stay in Love
Jude says to Pray in the Spirit and most people stop there at the end of that verse. But the sentence goes on, "and stays in Love". Love is the source of all we do. The combination of praying in the Spirit and the Love walk are powerful tools given to us on the inside. Want to be built up? Walk in love and pray in the Spirit. Study the Word on Spirit and Love and pray in the Spirit and the Spirit of Love.

Paul said in **Romans 14:19** in speaking of conduct to each other in love
"Lets us therefore make every effort to do what leads to peace and mutual edification."

1 Corinthians 10:24
Let no man seek his own, but every man another's wealth.
No one should seek his own good but the good of others. Put others before yourself.

Love places the emotional, physical and spiritual needs of others above itself. It gives as it can to others. God, who is Love, loved us so much that He Gave his best. Jesus

Love is the binding agent, the glue that holds the many parts of the body together even when it seems the parts do not fit together.

Love does not provide a stumbling block for others, if your actions are hurting or distressing another, you are no longer walking in love. Romans 14:15. Sometimes we need to put ourselves down for the good of others, even those we might think are lesser than us. If we exalt others, we will be exalted. Most folks are seeking to exalt themselves but those walking in love will look to exalt Him and then be exalted by Him. Two very different words there exalt and exalted. One is us exalting ourselves and the other is God exalting us.

Love Feasts

Churches until the 4th century held Love feasts, unlike the old Jewish feasts; they would hold Christian feasts, celebrations in honor of Jesus. They eventually

Became just like Jewish feasts where Pharisee and Sadducees would not eat together. They would separate rich from poor, and people quit making food for all and only for themselves. The feast went on for a few hundred years until they were persecuted by governments and not allowed to have them. And yet when you study the roots of the different Greek and Hebrew words used for love, you will find one definition that calls Agape "a love feast" A huge celebration of how much others and especially God means to us.

In 1 Corinthians 11:20, Paul rebukes them for getting drunk and providing their own family food instead of for all in common. Here Paul rebukes them for not having the feast but the manner they were doing it. They were no better than the Jews who turned the feasts of God into social events to promote and care only for themselves. Read Jude 12. Even Jude rebukes them at their feasts. Jude says their trees are without fruit they are dead. Where is the reason for the season? Their love feasts are just reasons to get drunk and pose as Christians.

In 2 Peter 2:12-13, he says that many have worked into their midst at the feasts posing as Christians, they destroy the fellowship of the love feast and bring dissension to the body. In these love feasts the rich sat apart from the poor and did not mingle with them. They despised the poor and then when they took the Lords Supper it brought on them sickness and disease.

Love does not separate itself from people of different races, income or stature. You cannot walk in love with out loving all.

1 John 4 7-12

7 Beloved, let us love one another: for love is of God; and every one that loveth is born of God, and knoweth God. 8 He that loveth not knoweth not God; for God is love. 9 In this was manifested the love of God toward us, because that God sent his only begotten Son into the world, that we might live through him. 10 Herein is love, not that we loved God, but that he loved us, and sent his Son to be the propitiation for our sins. 11 Beloved, if God so loved us, we ought also to love one another. 12 No man hath seen God at any time. If we love one another, God dwelleth in us, and his love is perfected in us.

You want people to know you know Jesus. You want folks to know you as a follower of Jesus. Walk in Love. Love all people and all types of people, even those with whom you do not agree. Love those who persecute you. Love those who look different – love them.

Racism is not from God and cannot be condoned in the Word.

Proof of Love

Romans 13: 8 & 9

8 Owe no man anything, but to love one another: for he that loveth another hath fulfilled the law. 9 For this, Thou shalt not commit adultery, Thou shalt not kill, Thou shalt not steal, Thou shalt not bear false witness, Thou shalt not covet; and if there be any other commandment, it is briefly comprehended in this saying, namely, Thou shalt love thy neighbour as thyself. 10 Love worketh no ill to his neighbour: therefore love is the fulfilling of the law.

You are not bound to brothers in obedience as you are civil leaders but you are bound by love. If we walk in love, make it a daily 24 hour practice, day by day we can fulfill the law. Walking in love is the fulfillment of the law. Any other method has and will always prove unsuccessful. Only

Love can meet the requirements of the law and the renewed law which was commanded by Jesus, to love God and our neighbors as ourselves. We tend to be selfish and if we loved others with that same selfish passion, we would change the life and world. If we protected others, others peoples families, looked after others as we do our own, we are loving them and fulfilling the law. We must look after others, which is the debt of love.

Recently I read a story about a young man who stopped to give elderly lady money on the street. He had given up his lunch to help this lady. A little later he was driving by again and he saw her driving away in a brand new car! He stopped her and he chewed her out. Unfortunately he made a sad confession later. He stated, "I will never help anyone again!" Sadly he was so blind by anger he has given up on love, on giving. It is more blessed to give than to receive. That experience possibly has caused him more damage because he allowed it to change and harden his heart. Yes the lady was as far as we know, wrong. Reacting the way the man did, did not hurt her but rather him and others he was meant to help down the road. The devil's trick worked. When someone does us wrong we do not change, we do not give up on love. We must keep walking in love no matter the appearance of what we see currently happening. Plant the seed and keep it in the ground with love.

The Proof that proves that you are born again is in it the Love you have... the love you possess and act on, rely on to live the "much more" life.

1 John 4:7- 14 THE TEST OF THE BORN AGAIN EXPERIENCE

John proves that we are of God in verse 7 and proves our sonship (read also 1John 5:1-2) Verses 7 and 8 is the proof of knowing God. Verse 8 tells us because God is love and we should imitate Him as His children (also Eph 5:1) Verse 9 tells us because God has imparted His love to us. (Rom 5:5) Verse 9 tells us that God sent His Son to make it all possible (also 1 Pt 2:21) Verse 9 also tells us that we might live, verse 10 tells us because God first loved and that we have been loved and forgiven of so much. Verse 11 tells us that God loved us when we were unlovable (Rm 5:6-10) Verse 12 tells us that God dwells in us and that His love is perfected in us and verse 13 that it is because of the indwelling Spirit. Verse 16 tells us that we believe in Love and dwell in Him, verse 17 tells us that we are like him and verse 20 proves we love Him.

Walking in Love is the command of Jesus (1 John 5:2) and it should be natural for the sons of God.

The giving of God's only begotten Son it the fullest proof of the infinite love of God and that all men can find full mercy in it. 1John 9-10 and John 3:16

Loving God and keeping His commandments are proof that we love the brethren (1 John 5:1-3, 1 John 2:9-11, 1John 3:14-16) and loving the brethren is proof that we love God (1 John 5:1-3, 1 John 3:17-18, 1 John 4:7-21) The proof of our relationship in Christ is not in what we preach, or say, or even do, but in how we love. That is both an action and verbal lifestyle that proves the love of God in us and we in Him.

While we were lost, He sought us, how much more so should we seek Him in return. If we have entered into the how much more so life, we need to act like we know it... If death reigned in us before and now life does... "how much more" should we be grateful and pursue the one who made a way for us a path of love and righteousness for us to follow.

Love is made perfect

1 John 4:17 God love is made perfect in us and brings us to perfection because it is the way of perfection. Paul said in 2:13 when perfection comes... that is love

With God dwelling in us and Love dwelling in us and our dwelling in Him we can know we can have the fullness of love (Eph 3:19) and that perfect love in daily manifestation we can have boldness at the throne of God and day of judgment.

If we continue dwelling in God and God can dwelling in us then God who is Love and perfect can dwell in us and we can then tap into that perfect way... the love way... recall John 14, I am the vine and you are the branch, any man who dwells in me... Rivers will flow... that same sap that flows through Jesus and up out of God flows through us, if we dwell in Him. We must stay in vital living contact with Him though. We cannot allow anything to break that love connection with Him. We must battle to stay in love and walk in love with all our hearts all our soul and all our strength. We must depend on him to supply the Love and just stay connected with Him. Let nothing break that connection... No sin, or weight that easily entangles (Heb 12:1)... pursue love and stay there (Jude 20&21)!

BROTHER JOHN

Rm 8:28 God works all things out for our good
Prepared for them that love him 1 Cor 2:9
Promised to him that love him Jas 1:12

Only AGAPE love in practice and as a noun, will satisfy the needs of the lost world -- and you and me. We need it more than we could ever know and if we would trust and rely in that Love. If we act in faith towards living a life of love the greatest quest of our lives, we would be radically different. We would fulfill the law, have a foundation that cannot be moved, be blameless and pure at His coming and conquer the world. I could go on for days about what love would produce in your life and mine if we wanted to. Everything we tell God we want and desire is wrapped up in the love walk. He told us in the beginning to Love Me with all your heart, all your soul and all your strength, then shall all this be added unto you. Jesus said "Seek ye first the kingdom of God and His righteousness and all this will be added unto you. Seek His kingdom, it is a kingdom of love and with that love relationship come all the needed resources to do what He has asked of us to do. Gives new meaning to the prodigal son story when you see it in the light of love. How many people are in the Church the house of God but not enjoying the benefits of that household because they misunderstand their Father? We have always had access to all God has, but we have been unwilling to walk in it, to walk in love. You make walking in love the focus and you will find you will have no issue living the Holy life, getting rid of sin, breaking strong holds, testing the spirit of others, knowing right from wrong, being Christ like, being mature, healing, wisdom and any other benefit you can think of that comes from a right standing relationship with God. Get right with God get right in Love. Root yourself in it and make it your life's journey.

Remember, God is a Spirit, God is Love, so are we taking a giant leap in stating that the Spirit is Love? Are they not the one and same?

THE HOW "MUCH MORE SO" LIFE

The more I study the more I find myself discovering that there is so much that God wants us to achieve. There is a place, a place that is so very close to God that being there causes us to act just like Him. This is what Jesus did when He lived among us. The world is hungry for it, but is the Church? I want so much of God that people take note I have been with Jesus. I have heard it said a number of times, "That person is so spiritual that they are of no earthly good". I don't know about you but I see that if I could be filled to the complete fullness of God and His love, I would be so spiritual that it would be of total earthly good. The World wants it, but they can't tell you what they need when they can't see it in anyone. How could you describe something that you need if you have never seen it? The world has no idea what it needs, it is blind, but we do.

I love the scripture in Romans 8:2

For the law of the Spirit of life in Christ Jesus hath made me free from the law of sin and death.

What is the law of the Spirit? Well is not the Spirit God and is God not Love? Did Jesus not say, a new command I give unto you "Love" He went on to say, all the law and the prophets hang on this one law, Love. The law of the Spirit is the Law of Love! We have been set free from the law of sin and death that could not satisfy the need of redemption or bring liberty to us and all of creation. The creation is waiting on us to begin to manifest the Law of Love and come into all we are to be. We are what the Word says we are even if others do not agree.

We have been set free to bring liberty to others! We have been set free to be the dwelling place of the presence of God in this world. We are the new mercy seat! We are the new tabernacle of God. We have the potential of God the awesome magnificent, wonderful everything in us!

God wants more for us than we can ever imagine. The prophet **Jeremiah** said

29: 11 For I know the thoughts that I think toward you, saith the Lord, thoughts of peace, and not of evil, to give you an expected end. 12 Then shall ye call upon me, and ye shall go and pray unto me, and I will hearken unto you. 13 And ye shall seek me, and find me, when ye shall search for me with all your heart.

God has great plans for us, but we need to quit looking at the end and focus on the journey at our feet right now. Focus on Him and your relationship with Him and let Him determine the path He has for you. No servant can be above His master, but many people start running and then ask God to bless them and yet God never told them to do it. Find out His plan and then stay in contact with Him every day to get the next step out of the boat. Once you step out of the boat the path will be hard and you will be walking when no man has done so before. You will be amazed by the plan He has. He wants only the best for His children, may not always be easy but it is always worth it.

God wants to see us arrive at a full satisfying place with Him and do all the He says in His Word we are suppose to do. Below are some Scriptures about what I call the "How much more life" from our great example Paul.

Romans 5:

9 Much more then, being now justified by his blood, we shall be saved from wrath through him. 10 For if, when we were enemies, we were reconciled to God by the death of his Son, much more, being reconciled, we shall be saved by his life.

In the NIV it says of both verses, "Since we have been justified by his blood, HOW MUCH MORE SO, shall we be saved from God's wrath through Him. 10 For if, when we were Gods enemies we were reconciled to him through the death of His son, HOW MUCH MORE SO, having been reconciled, shall we be saved through His life."

Romans 5:
15 But not as the offence, so also is the free gift. For if through the offence of one many be dead, much more the grace of God, and the gift by grace, which is by one man, Jesus Christ, hath abounded unto many.

17 For if by one man's offence death reigned by one; much more they which receive abundance of grace and of the gift of righteousness shall reign in life by one, Jesus Christ.)

How much more so will we reign in life through Jesus! Let us as Paul said, press on to the high calling of Jesus and at least attempt to hit the mark. Let us give it a go. We have nothing to lose. Think about how far we went in sin and death, then go the opposite direction in light and life to where God wants us to go. Get going, press into it. Discipline yourself to pray and study the Word and become that person the World and God is looking for. Be the answer the World does not even think exists. Step up and accept the greater life. The World thinks Jesus and that Acts of the Apostles is stuff of legends. People even say that Jesus was just a fairy tale or nursery rhyme. It is time for those of us with the right stuff to become and demonstrate that the legends are not dead.

We have a high calling, greater works to do. But we must be pressing into the grace of Jesus. We must pursue it with all we have. Love God with all our hearts and all our soul … give it our all and begin to live the how much more so life. If the glory on Moses was so great that they could not look upon him how much more so, should the Presence and Glory of God be on us?

It says that the glory of the latter house will be greater than the former in Haggai 2:9. If we are in the 7th day since Adam and the Third day since Jesus, we can't get much latter than that. What are you waiting for, jump into the "much more life."

John 14:
12 Verily, verily, I say unto you, He that believeth on me, the works

that I do shall he do also; and greater works than these shall he do; because I go unto my Father. 13 And whatsoever ye shall ask in my name, that will I do, that the Father may be glorified in the Son. 14 If ye shall ask any thing in my name, I will do it.

God has a great plan and He sent Jesus to show us how to do it and then let it be in our hands. We must be diligent to do the job of the church while also fulfilling the purpose of the church. He wants you and all of you. He wants you to be so full of Him you can change the way the world affects you. Raise up your eyes and see the Glory of the Lord as it comes. It is coming, prepare yourself so you can be a part of the greatest days on earth. You will see greater works because you are alive in the day it will happen, the real question is will you be part of them or a spectator?

Press in and discover the destiny that God has for you. Break free of the trappings of men and the world. As Paul said in Hebrews, throw off every weight and sin that easily besets you.. run my friend, be a man who runs so hard for God that the world has no idea what to say about you other then ..

Acts 4:
13 Now when they saw the boldness of Peter and John, and perceived that they were unlearned and ignorant men, they marveled; and they took knowledge of them, that they had been with Jesus.

I want to be known as one who spent time with Jesus. I do not want anything else that anyone else has. I want all that I can get of the presence of God. I want to know Him so well that I can make Him known to others and that they would catch the fire of the Spirit as well and run further, faster and higher than I could ever dream.

When we planted our church here we started from the get go with a vision for the lost. A vision to raise up laborers and send them from this small Central American country to the World. We began our church committing to give at least 51 percent of all that is given to missions. We take this vision serious and coupled with the Bible School we will send laborers to the nations.

We as a church will do all we have to keep the vision in front of the people God has drawn to us. We will not allow cares of the world to distract us and render us powerless and cold. If as pastor I am responsible

WHY ARE THE FISHERMEN EATING THE BAIT?

for the teaching, the money and the vision, I will give it away, teach as many as we can and broadcast that vision as far as I can. I will expend myself for the sake of the Gospel and this wonderful Love that course through my veins. I will give it my all and if the world laughs at us, so be it. I will give my all to feed the sheep as God has instructed, moving them to perfection and fullness and ultimately their own destiny. My success lies completely in preparing them and maturing them and sending them out into the world to change the way the world affects us.

We will not be moved by what the antichrist is doing or by what he thinks he can do to stop us. We do not focus on the world or their coming ruler. We focus on the mission and the Lord and will teach others to see that the Children of God do not live in fear and do not have any fear about the last days. I see this as our greatest hour! What the Word says about us and what we will do prevents us from being concerned about the false one. Many are glorying in the false one as they teach based on fear, exactly as he wants, that is the spirit of antichrist at work in the church. We teach on the manifestation and fullness of Christ in the Body and that is another book!

Please pursue Him, Follow after love and obtain the High calling in Christ, Maybe you are in an area that no one else sees it or understands it. Then be the one who changes the way the World affects you! Be the sign post they need to see it.

When He returns I pray that He finds my head in the Harvest field trying to grab one more for the Kingdom. Maybe He'll have to turn around and say, "Bro John, need a special invitation? You're going to miss the bus son." I'm not going to stop till the last possible second has expired. I will pursue Him with all I have and pray others do the same. I will have my head in the harvest looking for fruit. Maybe my friend, as I have with many others, we will meet somewhere in this ball of mud and fellowship for a few minutes before we go our ways to spread this fire and love.

So till we meet again at the great wedding feast!

May the grace of the lord Jesus Christ, the love of the Father and the fellowship of the Holy Spirit be with you!

www.ingramcontent.com/pod-product-compliance
Lightning Source LLC
Chambersburg PA
CBHW071754080526
44588CB00013B/2231